CASSEROLES

RYLAND
PETERS
& SMALL

LONDON NEW YORK

CASSEROLES
FROM GUMBO TO COQ AU VIN

Sonia Stevenson

photography by **William Lingwood**

First published in the United States in 2001
by Ryland Peters & Small, Inc.
519 Broadway, 5th Floor
New York, NY 10012
www.rylandpeters.com

Text © Sonia Stevenson 2001
Design and photographs
© Ryland Peters & Small 2001

10 9 8 7 6 5 4 3 2 1

Printed in China

Library of Congress
Cataloging-in-Publication Data

Stevenson, Sonia.
    Casseroles : from gumbo to coq au vin / Sonia
Stevenson ; photography by William Lingwood.
        p. cm.
    Includes index.
    ISBN 1-84172-209-X
    1. Casserole cookery. 2. Cookery, International.
I. Title.

TX693 .S82 2001
641.8'21--dc21   2001031880

For Patrick and Seren,
my Oldest and Youngest in the Family.

Author's acknowledgements

I am deeply grateful to Kai Wood and Sue, his wife,
for their help with the Chinese recipes; to Luc Votan,
for his assistance with Vietnamese and other dishes
from Southeast Asia; to my sister and brother-in-law
Gillian and Brenton Creelman in America, for their
help and patience; and last but certainly not least to
Elsa, my editor, for trying to keep me on the straight
and narrow and being an ever-ready source of help
in Times of Trouble.

Senior Designer Steve Painter
Commissioning Editor Elsa Petersen-Schepelern
Editor Susan Stuck
Indexer Hilary Bird
Production Meryl Silbert
Art Director Gabriella Le Grazie
Publishing Director Alison Starling

Food Stylist Julz Beresford
Assistant Food Stylist Christine Rodrigues
Stylist Antonia Gaunt
Photographer's Assistant Emma Bentham-Wood

Notes

All spoon measurements are level.

Fresh herbs are used in this book unless otherwise
stated. If using dried herbs, halve the quantity given.

Unsalted butter has been used in all the recipes. If
using salted butter, add a little less salt to the dish.

The oven should be preheated to the specified
temperature, except where indicated otherwise.

contents

The Casserole ...

No other word has ever been used to describe such a diverse variety of dishes. Try to define it in a few words and the explanation simply becomes longer and full of exceptions. It conjures up meat dishes, vegetable dishes, fish dishes, slow-cooked dishes, last-minute put-together dishes, gratins, curries, soups, modern dishes, old-fashioned traditional recipes, and so on. But they do have one thing in common. They are cooked in a simple, heatproof dish which could be called a casserole, even if it really is a tagine, hotpot, sandpot, or a daube—according to the part of the world in which you live.

As all these names suggest, there are many ways to cook a casserole, but most can be categorized by the technique used to make them.

A ragout is a basic stew with roux-thickened gravy. It comes in two forms, white and brown. White ones have white stock and meat and vegetables sautéed in hot butter without browning. Brown ones have meat and vegetables browned in fat, then flour is added and browned and the dish is then simmered in brown stock. In both cases, the cooking is long and slow and the vegetables are strained out and replaced with new ones as garnishes.

A fricassée is almost the same dish as a white ragout, but here the meat does not require long cooking and so any vegetables are served with the meat, while the gravy is often no more than a light, binding sauce. Egg yolks or arrowroot are often used as liaisons to thicken the sauce.

Braising is reserved for a large cut of meat or a whole chicken. The meat is browned in fat, a little liquid is added, and the whole is covered with a lid and sealed to prevent any steam escaping. Slow cooking is essential to prevent drying out and subsequent scorching. The American pot roast, some versions of the Indian *dum pukht,* and the French daube are good examples.

The poaching technique can be seen in fish stews of all kinds and many curries, especially those containing coconut milk or yogurt, which curdle when boiled. But perhaps the most famous of all are *Poule au Pot*, Chinese red-cooked dishes, *Pot au Feu,* or New England Boiled Dinner. The surface is skimmed from time to time and no thickening is used. The result is a dish of extraordinary tenderness.

In America, a casserole is sometimes understood to be an assembly of cooked or partially cooked food baked in an open dish topped with crumbs or herbs, as in Corn and Scallop Casserole (page 19), Provençal Tian (page 71), or Etouffée (page 16)—a cousin, perhaps, of the cassoulet. It is what, in other countries, might be called a "gratin."

So—in this exploration of the casseroles of the world, I've discovered that one cook's tagine is another's gumbo; one cook's braise is another's curry. Their similarities are just as exciting as their differences. There are many more marvelous dishes that could have been included, but these are my favorites.

"The history of every nation lies visible on its table." Nowhere is this quotation from one of Robert Carrier's books more true than of America. Its culinary history is a potpourri of dishes gleaned from the many cultures of its peoples, made with a cornucopia of ingredients produced by the world's most efficient agricultural system.

In America, it is said, you can get food from any part of the world, any time—either the authentic version, or its truly American descendant.

You want Italian? You have Cioppino—the famous fish stew invented in America by Italian-American fishing communities in California. It is endlessly adaptable, like similar seafood dishes anywhere.

You want French? America's great French cuisines are Creole and Cajun; the first a more sophisticated, city-based style of cooking, the second exuberant country food, both with echoes of African and Spanish influences. Gumbo, for instance, is named after the African word for "okra." There are many variations; made with chicken, seafood, duck, greens—and with or without the okra that gave it its name.

Probably one of the most famous American casseroles is Brunswick Stew, cooked in quantity for community gatherings for generations. Originally it included squirrel—and sometimes still does—but now is mostly made with chicken or rabbit. However, most casseroles—the braises, curries, ragouts, and stews in other sections of this book—have their American counterparts. There are just a few examples in this chapter. Try to discover more—they are inspiring.

THE AMERICAS

Cioppino

Versions of Cioppino are found all along the West Coast of America, wherever Italians settled: many have been fishermen there for generations. Most recipes seem to agree on one point: you must use a red wine. Some recipes use only shellfish and others insist on using only whole fish, with nothing filleted. However, the majority leave it to you to choose what's best locally.

To make the sauce, heat the olive oil in a large skillet, then add the onion, garlic, chiles, if using, and the chopped bell pepper. Sauté gently until softened but not browned, about 10 minutes. Add the wine, bring to a boil, and boil until the liquid is reduced to about ½ cup. Put the tomatoes in a blender and purée well. Transfer to the skillet, then add the tomato juice, fish stock or clam juice, salt, pepper, and fennel seeds. Bring to a boil again, reduce the heat, and simmer for 40 minutes.

Meanwhile, brush a 4-quart casserole with a thin coating of oil, then add the fish, cover with the boiling red wine sauce, and transfer to a preheated oven at 350°F for 15 minutes.

Remove from the oven and add the clams, shrimp, herbs, and a dash of Tabasco. Cover with a lid or foil and return to the oven for 10 minutes, or until all the shells have opened and the scallops are opaque. Very gently mix the fishes together.

Alternatively, cook the shellfish separately and fold them in after the fish has cooked, rejecting any that have not opened. Serve in large soup plates with plenty of hot garlic buttered baguettes—and finger bowls.

Variations Instead of the seafood, use 8 oz. haddock or halibut, 8 oz. peeled and deveined shrimp, 8 oz. mussels, 1 lb. clams, 8 oz. cooked crab, and 8 oz. scallops.

Alternatively, substitute 8 oz. fish such as halibut, 1 lb. shrimp, 1 lb. mussels, 10 oz. clams, about 24 limpets, 8 pieces of octopus, 8 small scallops, and 8 oz. crab pieces.

Note Make sure all the mussels have been scraped and rinsed, with the beards pulled away and discarded before cooking. Tap them against the kitchen counter and discard any that don't close. Clams should also close when tapped.

---

1 lb. firm white fish such as halibut, haddock, rockfish, or monkfish, cut into about 8 chunks

about 1 lb. clams or a mix of clams and mussels, rinsed and debearded

about 8 oz. uncooked shrimp, peeled and deveined but with tail fins intact

12 scallops, halved crosswise

2 tablespoons chopped fresh flat-leaf parsley

2 tablespoons chopped fresh cilantro or basil

a dash of Tabasco sauce

RED WINE SAUCE

⅓ cup olive oil

1 large onion, chopped

2 garlic cloves, crushed

2 jalapeño chiles, chopped (optional)

1 red or orange bell pepper, halved, seeded, and chopped

2 cups red wine

6 ripe tomatoes, peeled, seeded, and chopped

2 cups tomato juice

½ cup fish stock (page 140) or clam juice

1 teaspoon salt

¼ teaspoon freshly ground black pepper

¼ teaspoon fennel seeds

SERVES 4

Shrimp and Okra Gumbo

Gumbos are true Creole cooking: their main characteristic is that the flour is always browned slowly to a chestnut color—a roux. As the word gumbo means "okra" in some parts of Africa, you would think that the dish should always include that vegetable. Well, some do and some don't—and this one "do." Originally gumbo was a Lenten dish, without even the shellfish, but later, fish and seafood were added and sometimes chicken too. This was served at a later meal, but left a delicious taste in the stock.

Shrimp and Okra Gumbo
step-by-step

1 bunch of watercress, washed and trimmed

1 bunch of parsley, washed and trimmed

1 bunch of spinach, washed and trimmed

10 scallions, green ends only

1 bunch of chard or beet greens, washed and trimmed

1 lb. uncooked, unpeeled shrimp

4 cups chicken stock (page 134) or water

1 sprig of thyme

1 sprig of marjoram

2 bay leaves

5 whole allspice berries

1½ tablespoons butter or peanut oil

2 tablespoons all-purpose flour

2 garlic cloves, crushed

1 onion, chopped

½ teaspoon cayenne pepper

4 crab claws

8 oz. andouille sausage, cut in ½-inch slices (optional)

2–3 dozen clams and/or mussels, well scrubbed and debearded if necessary

8–12 medium okra

1 teaspoon Tabasco sauce

SERVES 4

1 Pour 2 cups lightly salted water into a large saucepan and bring to a boil. Press in the watercress, parsley, spinach, scallions, and chard or beet greens. Cover and cook until just tender, about 5 minutes. Strain through a colander, reserving the cooking water. Chop the greens and set aside.

2 To make the stock, peel the shrimp and put the shells and heads, if any, into a large saucepan or casserole dish. Add the reserved cooking water, stock or water, thyme, marjoram, bay leaves, and allspice. Simmer for 15 minutes and set aside.

6 Add the crab claws to the casserole, then add the reserved hot stock. Add the andouille, if using. Bring to a boil.

7 Add the clams, return to a boil, then simmer, covered, for about 15 minutes or until the clams open.

Meanwhile, to prepare the okra, trim minimally around the stalk end, without cutting into the middle.

3 Strain the stock into a saucepan, return to a boil, reduce the heat, and keep the stock warm.

4 Meanwhile, heat the butter or oil in a large casserole dish or Dutch oven, add the flour and sauté very slowly until the flour becomes a hazelnut color, about 10 minutes: do not let the butter burn.

5 Add the garlic, onion, and cayenne pepper and sauté for 2 minutes.

8 As the clams open (they will do so in stages), remove them to a plate with a slotted spoon. This will stop them overcooking. Add the okra to the pan.

9 Return the reserved chopped greens to the casserole and bring to a boil. Add a dash of Tabasco sauce.

10 Share the seafood, okra, and greens between 4 large bowls, ladle the stock over the top, then serve with steamed white rice.

Shrimp Etouffée

6 tablespoons butter,
plus 2 tablespoons extra (see note)

¼ cup all-purpose flour

1 large onion, chopped finely

1 green bell pepper, seeded and diced

1 celery stalk, sliced

1 garlic clove, crushed

6 scallions, coarsely sliced

¼ teaspoon cracked black pepper

¼ teaspoon cayenne pepper

a pinch of ground cumin

a large pinch of hot red
pepper flakes, or to taste

1¼ cups fish stock (page 140)

1 tablespoon chopped fresh
flat-leaf parsley

1 teaspoon lemon juice

2 lb. peeled, uncooked shrimp

SERVES 4

The smell of butter and flour browning slowly in a large iron pot. The sizzle of freshly chopped onions, green bell peppers, and scallions added at just the right moment as the flour and butter turn a rich brown—all cooked in the dark roux. This is real, smoky-flavored Cajun cooking. Often this dish is made with crawfish, which are plentiful in the waters of Louisiana, but I have made it with shrimp. Etouffée means "smothered"—the dish is smothered by being covered with a lid, and the shrimp cook gently in the steamy atmosphere.

Heat the butter in a heavy, flameproof casserole dish and mix in the flour. Stir it steadily for 3 minutes over high heat so it first loses its moisture, then starts to take on a little color. Immediately turn the heat to very low and continue stirring. Very gradually, both the flour and the butter will turn a rich chestnut-brown color with a delicious cookie-like flavor. This will take at least 12 minutes.

To stop the flour browning any further, stir in the onion, bell pepper, celery, garlic, and half the scallions. Cook at medium heat until softened, then add the cracked pepper, cayenne, cumin, pepper flakes, stock, and extra butter (see note below).

Bring to a boil, beat until smooth, then taste and adjust the seasoning. Simmer for 15 minutes for the sauce to mature. Just before serving, add the remaining scallions, parsley, lemon juice, and finally the shrimp. Bring to a boil, cover tightly with a lid or foil, and cook very gently for 5 minutes, or until the shrimp are opaque all the way through. The time will vary according to the size of the shrimp. Do not overcook.

Serve over hot fluffy rice.

Note For best flavor, use shrimp butter instead of regular butter. You need shrimp shells, so buy unpeeled shrimp. Melt 1¼ sticks butter in a saucepan, add ½ cup water and the shrimp shells, and boil for 15 minutes. Strain and chill. The butter will form a hard layer on the surface, which can be removed and used in this and other seafood recipes.

A casserole from Chesapeake Bay where scallops and oysters are relatively cheap, though it could just as well come from anywhere on the East Coast, from Maine to South Carolina. The word "casserole" in American cooking is sometimes used to describe a dish of meats, fish, and/or vegetables, bound by a rich sauce, and topped with crumbled crackers or breadcrumbs, then browned in an oven or under a broiler, as in this recipe.

3 ears fresh corn
or 2 cups frozen corn, thawed

1 cup cooked rice
(from ¼ cup raw rice)

4 tablespoons butter

½ red bell pepper,
seeded and diced

1 red chile, finely sliced

3 scallions, white and
green parts, sliced

about 12 large scallops, halved
crosswise, or 16–20 shucked fresh
oysters, with their liquor

1 teaspoon celery salt or salt

¼ teaspoon cracked black pepper

2 tablespoons fish stock
(page 140) or water

½ cup heavy cream

2–3 egg yolks, beaten

TOPPING

4 tablespoons butter

1 cup fresh breadcrumbs

sweet paprika, for dusting

*4 heavy china teacups or ramekins,
or a 4-cup gratin dish, buttered*

SERVES 4

Fresh Corn and Scallop Casserole

If using fresh corn, cut the kernels off the cob with a sharp knife. Put the corn in a large saucepan of boiling salted water, blanch for 1 minute, then drain. Mix the corn with the cooked rice.

Melt the butter in a skillet, add the diced bell pepper, chile, and scallions, and stir-fry for about 2 minutes until aromatic. Transfer to a plate.

Add the scallops or oysters to the skillet and stir-fry for about 30 seconds to firm them a little. Season with salt and pepper, then divide them between the cups or ramekins. Spoon the corn-and-rice mixture over the top, then top with the reserved red pepper, chile, and scallions.

Melt the butter for the topping in a small skillet, add the breadcrumbs, then sauté for a few minutes until the crumbs are lightly golden.

Put the stock, cream, and egg yolks in a bowl, together with any liquor from the oysters, if using, and beat lightly with a fork. Pour into the cups or ramekins.

Top with the breadcrumbs, sprinkle with paprika, and cook in a preheated oven at 425°F for 10 minutes. Brown the top under the broiler if necessary, then serve.

This is a very simple recipe, so make the most of it with top-quality, kosher chicken. The dumplings are cooked on top of the casserole so that they expand and stick together, forming a sort of lid on top. You can also cook them simply in a saucepan of boiling salted water.

Lemon Chicken with Dumplings

4 chicken breasts

2 cloves

1 bay leaf

10 peppercorns

2 celery stalks, sliced

½ onion, sliced

1 carrot, sliced

1 cup chicken stock (page 134)

MARINADE

shredded zest and juice of 1 lemon

½ teaspoon salt dissolved in ½ cup water

DUMPLING MIX

3 cups all-purpose flour

1 teaspoon salt

2 tablespoons baking powder

1 tablespoon chopped fresh
flat-leaf parsley (optional)

2 eggs, beaten

2 tablespoons butter, melted,
plus 1 tablespoon extra, to glaze

¼ cup milk

SERVES 4

Mix the marinade ingredients in a shallow dish. Slice each chicken breast into 3 long strips, add to the dish, cover, and chill for 4 hours or overnight.

Reserve the chicken breasts and transfer the marinating liquid to a flameproof casserole. Tie the cloves, bay leaf, and peppercorns in a little cheesecloth bag for easy removal later, then add to the casserole. Add the celery, onion, carrot, and chicken stock. Bring to a boil on top of the stove, then reduce the heat and simmer for 20 minutes.

Meanwhile, to make the dumplings, sift the flour, salt, and baking powder into a mixing bowl, then stir in the herbs, if using. Make a well in the center of the flour, add the egg, the 2 tablespoons melted butter, and milk, and stir with a wooden spoon until a soft ball forms. Do not overwork the mixture or the dumplings will become heavy when cooked. Divide the dough into 16 small balls and set aside. About 15 minutes before serving, drop the dumplings into a large saucepan of boiling salted water and return to a boil. Reduce the heat and simmer for 5 minutes. Carefully turn them over with a slotted spoon and continue simmering for a further 5 minutes. Using the slotted spoon, transfer them to a plate, and glaze with the remaining melted butter. Cover with plastic wrap to prevent them drying out. Keep them warm.

Remove the cheesecloth bag from the casserole. Put the marinated chicken pieces into the casserole on top of the vegetables, then arrange the dumplings on top. Bring to a boil on top of the stove, then transfer to a preheated oven and cook at 400°F for 20 minutes. Put under a preheated broiler for about 3 minutes if you would like to brown the dumplings. Serve in the casserole.

A creamy, colorful dish with a beautiful aroma of herbs and fresh corn. It originates in New Orleans, where the Cajun word *maquechoux* means "smothered in corn," which it certainly is! And what else would you serve with it other than a quick cornbread!

Chicken Maquechoux
with Cornbread

⅓ cup corn or peanut oil

1 chicken, cut into serving pieces

½ teaspoon salt

2 onions, finely chopped

2 ears fresh corn

1 green bell pepper, seeded and finely chopped

2 tomatoes, peeled and seeded

2 sprigs of thyme

½ cup whipping cream

1 tablespoon fresh basil, chopped

CORNBREAD

1 cup yellow cornmeal

1 cup all-purpose flour

1 tablespoon sugar

4 teaspoons baking powder

1 teaspoon salt

a pinch of ground allspice

a pinch of ground white pepper

1 large egg

1 cup milk

¼ cup vegetable shortening, plus 1½ tablespoons extra (or bacon fat), for greasing

SERVES 4

To make the cornbread, sift the dry ingredients into a mixing bowl. Add the egg, milk, and the ¼ cup shortening. Beat with a wooden spoon until smooth, about 1 minute.

Grease a 9-inch ovenproof skillet with the remaining shortening or bacon fat, pour in the batter, and bake in a preheated oven at 425°F for 25 minutes until golden brown on top. Remove from the oven and cut into wedges.

To cook the chicken, heat 3 tablespoons of the oil in a nonstick skillet, add the chicken pieces, and sauté until brown, turning them often and seasoning them with salt.

Heat the remaining oil in a heavy flameproof casserole, add the onion and 2 tablespoons water, and cook until softened but not browned. (The water will help the onion cook without browning or using too much butter.)

Meanwhile, strip the corn from the cobs with a knife, cutting downwards from end to end and scraping any bits left behind. Add the corn to the casserole, then add the chopped peppers, tomatoes, thyme, and a little more seasoning. Bring to a boil, then reduce to a simmer for 5 minutes to combine the flavors. Add the cream, bring to a boil, and reduce a little of the liquid which the corn gives off.

Transfer the browned pieces of chicken to the casserole. Cook, uncovered, in a preheated oven at 375°F until the chicken juices run clear when pricked with a fork, about 35 minutes. Stir in the basil and return the casserole to the oven for a further 5 minutes. Serve with the cornbread on the side.

Note For moist interior and crisp crust, you need a steamy oven atmosphere. Put a dish two-thirds filled with water on the floor of your oven before you begin to cook the cornbread. This clever trick works well with many home-baked breads.

2 ducks, about 3 lb. each

¼ cup all-purpose flour

2 cups chicken stock (page 134)

1 cup beef stock (page 136)

3 tablespoons red currant jelly

½ cup sweet sherry

½ cup sherry vinegar

1 tablespoon sugar

2 teaspoons crushed garlic

2 sprigs of fresh thyme

1 tablespoon chopped
fresh flat-leaf parsley

salt and freshly ground black pepper

SERVES 4

Cut each duck into 4, giving 8 pieces in all.

Heat a dry, nonstick skillet. Working in batches if necessary, add the duck pieces, skin side down, and cook over a medium heat until well browned. Lots of the fat will run out, so pour it off into a bowl from time to time.

Set the breasts aside and put the legs in a flameproof casserole with a lid.

Pour off all but 3 tablespoons of the duck fat in the skillet, add the flour, and cook very slowly over a medium heat to a deep chestnut color.

Add the stocks and bring to a boil, stirring all the time to make a smooth sauce. Add the jelly, sherry, sherry vinegar, sugar, garlic, and herbs and continue stirring until the red currant jelly has dissolved.

Add a pinch of salt, then pour the mixture over the duck legs in the casserole. Bring to a boil on top of the stove, reduce to a simmer, and cook for 1 hour. Add the duck breasts and continue cooking for a further 45 minutes.

Taste and adjust the seasoning, then serve.

Creole Duck

A typical Creole recipe with roux—deeply browned flour—plus the trinity of Creole flavorings; garlic, thyme, and parsley. The sauce in which the duck cooks has a tantalizing, slightly sweet-sour overtone which cuts the richness of duck.

Yankee Pot Roast
with Braised Root Vegetables

The pot roast is one of the great American classics—
and when it appears with braised vegetables, it becomes
Yankee Pot Roast. You can also roast the vegetables
instead of braising.

2 lb. boneless beef chuck
or rump roast, neatly tied

3 tablespoons oil or bacon fat

1 tablespoon ground allspice

1 teaspoon salt

2 tablespoons all-purpose flour

1 tablespoon dry mustard

⅔ cup red wine

2 cups beef stock (page 136)

6 tablespoons butter

4 parsnips, cut into 2-inch chunks

2 sweet potatoes,
cut into 2-inch chunks

2 carrots, cut into 2-inch chunks

12 small red onions, cut into 4 wedges
through the root

2 tablespoons cornstarch

salt and freshly ground black pepper

SERVES 4

Put the meat in a shallow dish. Put 1 tablespoon of the oil,
allspice, salt, flour, and mustard in a small bowl and mix to
form a paste, adding more oil as necessary. Rub the meat
with the mixture, cover, and marinate in the refrigerator for
3 hours or overnight.

Remove the meat and shake off any excess spices. Heat the
remaining oil or bacon fat in a large skillet, add the meat, and
brown on all sides. Transfer to an ovenproof casserole.

Add the wine to the skillet, bring to a boil, and cook until
reduced by two-thirds. Add the stock and bring to a boil, pour
over the meat, cover with a lid, and cook in a preheated oven
at 350°F for 1½ hours or until tender.

Add the butter to the skillet, heat gently, then add the
vegetables and sauté until they take on a little color. Sprinkle
with salt and pepper, cover with a lid, and simmer in their own
juices for 20 minutes. Keep them warm.

When the meat is cooked, drain off the liquid into a saucepan.
Mix the cornstarch with 3 tablespoons water and blend it into
the liquid. Bring to a boil and check the seasoning. Pour the
sauce back over the meat and vegetables and heat on top
of the stove.

To serve, transfer the meat to a platter and arrange the
reheated vegetables around. Serve the gravy separately.

Chili con Carne

This Texan classic is one of the most satisfying dishes of all and is justly world famous. Chili con Carne is almost always made with chili powder, but I also like to make it with hot red pepper flakes or sliced fresh chiles. For timid tastebuds, adjust the quantity of chiles or chili powder to suit.

Be sure to boil those beans well! Red kidney beans should be boiled hard for 15 minutes at the beginning of the cooking time. I then discard the water and cover them with fresh water before proceeding with the recipe.

Remember, don't salt dried beans until towards the end of cooking time, otherwise they will be tough and take at least twice as long to cook. You can, of course, use the canned variety, but use the liquid from the can in the gravy if you do—it's part of the thickening.

Like most beans, other than fava beans, red kidney beans are native to the Americas—to Mexico, in fact. Smoky and delicious in flavor, their more elegant cousins are the white cannellini and the infant green flageolets.

Chili con Carne
step-by-step

2½ cups dried red kidney beans, washed

½ teaspoon salt

2 tablespoons shortening, corn oil, or beef drippings

2 onions, sliced

3 garlic cloves, sliced

2 lb. beef chuck, cut into ½-inch cubes

2 tablespoons all-purpose flour

2 tablespoons tomato paste

¼–½ tablespoon chili powder, dried chile flakes, or 1–4 whole red serrano chiles, seeded if preferred, then chopped

1 green bell pepper, halved, seeded, and chopped

¼ teaspoon ground cumin

4 cups beef stock

salt, to taste

TO SERVE
a little chopped cilantro

sour cream (optional)

flour tortillas, warmed, or crackers

SERVES 4–6

1 Put the beans in a bowl, cover with cold water, and let soak for at least 3 hours or overnight.* When ready to cook, drain, then rinse in cold water.

*If short of time, put them in a saucepan, cover with cold water, bring to a boil, simmer for 2 minutes, remove from the heat, cover, and let soak for 1 hour. Drain.

2 Put the beans in a saucepan, cover with cold water, bring to a boil, and boil hard for 15 minutes. Drain, cover with fresh water, and return to a boil. Simmer for 1–4 hours or until tender (the time depends on the age of the beans): top up with boiling water as necessary. Add ½ teaspoon salt 15 minutes before the end of cooking. Set aside.

3 Put the shortening, oil, or drippings in a large skillet and heat until melted. Add the onion and garlic and cook gently until softened and lightly browned, about 15 minutes. Transfer to a plate and keep them warm.

4 Add the beef cubes to the skillet, in batches if necessary—do not crowd the pan. Sauté until browned on all sides.

5 Stir in the flour and mix well.

6 Add the tomato paste, chili powder, hot red pepper flakes or fresh chiles, bell pepper, cumin, and stock and strain in any cooking liquid from the cooked beans or the liquid from the can, if using canned beans. Bring to a boil, transfer to a flameproof casserole dish or saucepan, and simmer on top of the stove or in a preheated oven at 300°F for 1¼ hours, or until the meat is tender.

7 Remove from the oven, season to taste, stir in the beans, return to the oven, and cook for a further 30 minutes.

8 Sprinkle with chopped cilantro and serve with a spoonful of sour cream, if using, and warmed tortillas or crackers.

Brunswick Stew

Taking its name from Brunswick County in Virginia, this is a dish designed for a large number of hungry people: it's not sophisticated, just full of goodness. The main ingredients are chicken, ham, and beef foreshank cut in the same way as osso buco, which could be used instead. (I was fascinated to discover that squirrel used to be one of the ingredients—now that's something that would scare some people!) Traditionally, the stew was thickened with mashed potatoes, but, in this modern version, they are served separately.

1 kg chicken, cut in 4, or 4 leg portions

1 ham bone or uncooked smoked pork hock

1½ lb. shank crosscuts of beef or osso buco

1 bay leaf

7 cups ham stock or water

1 onion, sliced

1 lb. tomatoes, halved, seeded, and chopped

1 celery heart, about 8 oz., chopped

8 oz. green baby lima (butter beans) or fava beans, about 1½ cups

1½ tablespoons chopped fresh basil

1½ tablespoons chopped fresh flat-leaf parsley

1 ear fresh corn (optional)

1 red serrano chile, seeded and sliced

1 teaspoon cracked black pepper

salt

buttery mashed potatoes, to serve

SERVES 8–10

Put the chicken, ham bone or hock, beef, and bay leaf into a large Dutch oven or casserole and cover with the stock or water. Do not season unless the hock is unsalted. Cover with a lid, bring to a boil, then reduce the heat, and simmer for about 40 minutes.

Lift out the chicken pieces and ham bone or hock and transfer to a large plate. Let cool and then cut off their meat in chunks and set aside. Discard the bones.

Continue simmering until the beef comes away from the center bone, about 2–4 hours. Discard the bone and add the beef to the chicken and hock.

If necessary, reduce the pan juices to about 3½ cups by boiling hard, then add the onions, tomatoes, celery, lima or fava beans, basil, and parsley. Cover and simmer for about 20 minutes until done.

Return the meats to the casserole. If using corn, strip the kernels from the cob and add them to the casserole. Add the chile and pepper, simmer for 5 minutes, taste, and adjust the seasoning. Serve with lots of mashed potatoes.

¼ cup corn, canola, or safflower oil

2 onions, finely chopped

1–2 fresh red chiles

2 garlic cloves, crushed

1 teaspoon chopped fresh oregano

1 teaspoon ground cumin

1 teaspoon Tabasco sauce

1 teaspoon sweet paprika

a pinch of cayenne pepper

1 cup canned chopped tomatoes
(half a 16-oz. can)

½ teaspoon salt

1 lb. greens, such as collard or
mustard greens

1 lb. spinach, well rinsed

8 oz. green beans (1½ cups)

1 cucumber, peeled and cubed

HOMINY CAKES

2½ cups cooked fine hominy grits

2 tablespoons all-purpose flour,
plus extra for coating

1 egg

1 teaspoon sweet paprika

1 egg, beaten

¼ cup chopped fresh flat-leaf parsley

2 tablespoons butter

2 tablespoons peanut oil

salt and freshly ground black pepper

SERVES 4

Vegetarian Green Chili
with Hominy Cakes

Cook the hominy according to the directions on the package. If you prefer, you can make these cakes using cooked polenta instead, which, like hominy, is another ground corn product. Both make an excellent base for a fiery sauce like this.

To make the Chili, heat the oil in a skillet, add the onions, chiles, and garlic, and sauté until softened. Add the oregano and cumin and cook for 2 minutes, then add the Tabasco, paprika, cayenne, tomatoes, and salt. Simmer for 5 minutes.

Bring a large saucepan of salted water to a boil, add the greens, and cook for about 10 minutes, adding the spinach for the last 2 minutes, just until wilted. Remove all the greens from the water, drain, and squeeze dry. Arrange in a large oval baking dish. Blanch the beans and cucumber in the same boiling water for 2 minutes, then drain and distribute evenly over the greens.

Pour the sauce over the greens and simmer in a preheated oven 400°F for 20 minutes.

To make the Hominy Cakes, put the cooked grits in a bowl, stir in the flour, egg, paprika, salt, and pepper. Make hamburger-sized patties from the mixture, patting them between your palms. Dip the cakes first in beaten egg, then in the chopped parsley, then in flour. Heat the butter and oil in a wide skillet. Add the hominy cakes and sauté on both sides until golden brown. Serve on heated plates with the chili greens on top.

Caribbean Vegetable Stew

"Spicy mixtures of island vegetables, bound with tomatoes and red hot chiles"—a perfect description of many vegetable dishes in the Caribbean. In Jamaica, callaloo leaves would be used instead of spinach—and the root of the same plant is a yam known as dasheen. I've used sweet potato as a substitute. A plantain is a large cooking banana (some have delightful pale pink flesh), but you can use ordinary green bananas instead.

Put the oil in a large, flameproof casserole, add the onion, and cook until softened and translucent. Add the allspice, cumin, nutmeg, chiles, garlic, ginger, tomatoes, and parsley and cook to a sauce. Season with the soy sauce. Add the sweet potato, red onions, and plantains or bananas, cover, and simmer for 20 minutes, then add the carrots and spinach and cook for a further 5 minutes, adding the snowpeas for the last 2 minutes. Season, scatter with chives, then serve.

¼ cup canola or safflower oil

1 onion, chopped

2 teaspoon ground allspice

1 teaspoon ground cumin

¼ teaspoon freshly grated nutmeg

4 fresh red chiles, seeded and chopped

4 garlic cloves, crushed

2 inches fresh ginger, peeled and grated

5 tomatoes, peeled, seeded, and diced

1 tablespoon chopped fresh flat-leaf parsley

2 tablespoons soy sauce

1 sweet potato, peeled and cubed

2 red onions, quartered

2 plantains or green bananas, peeled and cut into chunks

6 baby carrots, trimmed

4 cups baby spinach, rinsed

1 cup snowpeas

freshly ground black pepper

snipped fresh chives, to serve

SERVES 4

Europe has more variations of the casserole than anywhere else. Ragout or *pot au feu*, navarin or hotpot, tian or *pochoise*—all are forms of casserole, often given the name of the vessel in which they are cooked.

Some, like the Steak and Kidney Pudding, are cooked in an "all-in-one" method with no preliminary browning of the ingredients. Others, like *Coq au Vin*, need more sophisticated treatment: the bird is browned in butter and the dark gravy enriched with reduced red wine.

At one time, a stock was kept simmering in a large cauldron over an open fire. A pot containing all the necessary casserole ingredients was suspended inside the cauldron, surrounded by the liquid, and the stew was "jugged." This method of very slow cooking is replicated both in the French bain-marie system and the modern slow cooker, where the temperature is kept significantly below boiling point, but high enough to cook protein.

Many of these recipes were originally cooked over an open fire of peat or wood. Later on, when people still did not have ovens in their own houses, but village bakeries did, long, slow cooking was done after the bread had been made, often on a falling temperature and making use of all the latent heat left in a solid fuel oven.

Closed ovens in kitchen ranges have come on the scene only in the past two hundred years or so, but have revolutionized casserole cooking everywhere.

But Europe, to my mind, is still the casserole capital of the world. Her people, intrepid travellers all—and determined colonizers—have taken with them the dishes of their homelands to every continent, from the Americas to Africa, from India to Australia.

EUROPE

A creamy, garlicky, fish stew that's a meal on its own. It is quite different from its sister soup, the bouillabaisse: it is made without tomato, but instead with a rich liaison of egg yolks and mayonnaise beaten in at the end. Traditionally, it would include fish such as whiting, monkfish, porgy, red gurnard (sea robin), conger eel, and whatever else was fresh and firm on the day.

La Bourride

1 tablespoon olive oil

1 onion, sliced

1 fennel bulb, sliced

3 garlic cloves, sliced

peeled zest of ½ orange

1 fresh bouquet garni (sprigs of parsley, thyme, bay leaf and celery, tied up with kitchen twine)

1 cup white wine

6 cups fish stock (page 140)

at least 3 lb. white fish, cut into large pieces (see recipe introduction)

4 egg yolks

1 garlic clove, crushed

¼ cup olive oil

salt and freshly ground black pepper

TO SERVE
boiled potatoes or triangles of white bread, toasted

SERVES 4

Heat the oil in a large, flameproof casserole, add the onion, fennel, garlic, orange zest, and bouquet garni, and sauté for 5 minutes without browning.

Add the wine, then bring to a boil until reduced to about 2–3 tablespoons. Add the stock, bring to a boil, then season with salt and plenty of pepper.

Carefully add the pieces of fish, cover with a lid, transfer to a preheated oven, and cook at 350°F for about 20–25 minutes. Remove from the oven and carefully drain the liquid into a large saucepan. Keep the fish warm in the casserole, but remove the bouquet garni.

Taste the liquid and, if the flavor isn't strong enough, bring to a boil and simmer until reduced to about 3½ cups.

Put the egg yolks and garlic into a small food processor or bowl, then gradually work in the olive oil, drop by drop, to form a thick mayonnaise. Gradually beat the mixture into the fish stock. Still stirring, bring the mixture almost to a boil (do not let it boil, or the eggs will scramble).

Remove from the heat, then strain the sauce back over the fish in the casserole. Serve with boiled potatoes or the traditional accompaniment of crisp toast.

There may seem a lot of mustard in this sauce, but, when you cook mustard, it loses its heat and you are left with a delicious flavor which no one can quite place once the poaching liquid has been added.

Traditional Fish Pie

2 cups milk

1½ lb. finnan haddie or fresh haddock, skinned

2¾ sticks unsalted butter

1 tablespoon dry mustard powder

¼ cup all-purpose flour

2 hard-cooked eggs, peeled and quartered

2 lb. baking potatoes

salt and freshly ground black pepper

SERVES 4

Put the milk in a wide saucepan, heat just to boiling point, then add the fish. Turn off the heat and let poach until opaque—do not overcook.

Meanwhile, melt 1¼ sticks of the butter in another saucepan, then stir in the mustard and flour. Remove from the heat and strain the poaching liquid into the pan.

Arrange the fish and eggs in a shallow pie dish or casserole.

Return the pan to the heat and, whisking vigorously to smooth out any lumps, bring the mixture to a boil. Season with salt and pepper if necessary. (Take care: if you are using smoked fish, it may be salty enough.) Pour the sauce into the casserole and mix carefully with the fish and eggs.

Cook the potatoes in boiling salted water until soft, then drain. Return to the pan. Melt the remaining 1½ sticks butter in a small saucepan. Reserve ¼ cup of this butter and stir the remainder into the potatoes. Mash well and season with salt and pepper. Spoon the mixture carefully over the sauced fish, brush generously with the reserved butter, and transfer to a preheated oven at 400°F for 20 minutes, or until nicely browned.

Note If no finnan haddie is available, add 4 oz. smoked salmon, finely sliced, sprinkled over the poached fish just before adding the sauce.

France's most famous stew is *Coq au Vin* (chicken in wine). To be authentic, it should contain mushrooms, bacon lardons, and caramelized baby onions. In the old days, when *coqs* were old cocks, the bird was simmered in red wine for hours, like a daube. Now it is nearly impossible to get an old bird, so modern recipes use a young bird and a shorter cooking time.

Coq au Vin

1 large chicken, preferably free-range or corn-fed, cut into serving pieces

leaves from 1 sprig of thyme, finely chopped

4 tablespoons butter

⅓ cup brandy

1 bottle rich red wine, 750 ml

3 cups chicken stock (page 134)

4 tomatoes, peeled and seeded, or 2 teaspoons tomato paste

2 garlic cloves, crushed

1 bay leaf

salt and freshly ground black pepper

ROUX
4 tablespoons butter
2 tablespoons all-purpose flour

TO SERVE
4 oz. thick-cut bacon, diced
1¼ sticks butter
1 cup button mushrooms, sliced
12 baby onions

SERVES 4

Season the chicken pieces with salt and pepper and sprinkle with the thyme. Put the butter into a large, flameproof casserole or Dutch oven and heat until it begins to brown. Add the chicken to the casserole and sauté, skin side down, until golden brown.

Remove the casserole from the heat, pour over the brandy, and set it alight if you wish—otherwise let it boil away so the alcohol evaporates. Using tongs or a slotted spoon, remove the chicken to a plate and keep it warm.

Pour the wine into the casserole, bring to a boil, and reduce to about 3–4 tablespoons. Add the tomatoes or paste, garlic, and bay leaf and mix well.

To make the roux, heat the butter in a small skillet, add the flour, and cook, stirring, until the mixture is a pale brown. Stir it into the mixture in the casserole.

Reserve 1 cup of the stock, stir the remainder into the casserole, and bring to a boil. Add the chicken and any juices that have run onto the plate. Season to taste, cover with a lid, and cook in a preheated oven at 350°F for 40 minutes, or until the chicken juices run clear when pricked with a fork.

Meanwhile, bring a saucepan of water to a boil, add the bacon, boil for 1 minute, then drain. Add the bacon into the casserole halfway through the cooking time.

Put 6 tablespoons of the serving butter in a small skillet, add the mushrooms, and sauté for 5 minutes. Transfer to the casserole for the last 5 minutes of cooking time.

Add the remaining butter to the skillet, add the onions, and sauté until browned, about 5 minutes. Add the reserved 1 cup chicken stock, bring to a boil, and simmer until tender and the stock has been absorbed, about 10 minutes.

Serve on heated dinner plates, topping each serving a share of the mushrooms, bacon, and golden onions.

Avgolémono—the liaison of egg yolks and lemon juice stirred into a dish before serving—is one of the hallmarks of Greek cooking. It produces a creamy texture without the heaviness of cream, as well as a refreshing effect which counteracts any richness.

Creamy Greek Lemon Chicken

4 tablespoons butter

2 tablespoons olive oil

3 lb. chicken, cut into serving pieces, or 3 lb. chicken pieces

1 onion, sliced

1 carrot, sliced

1 small celery stalk or slice of fennel, cut into chunks

2½ cups chicken stock (page 134)

1 tablespoon cornstarch

2 egg yolks

2 tablespoons fresh lemon juice

salt and freshly ground black pepper

TO SERVE

zest of 1 lemon, cut into fine strips or removed with a zester

sprigs of dill or 1 tablespoon chopped fresh dill

SERVES 4

Heat the butter and oil in a large, flameproof casserole. Season the chicken pieces, onion, carrot, and celery or fennel, add them to the casserole, and sauté gently without browning, but turning them over from time to time, about 15 minutes.

Add the stock, bring to a boil, then season to taste. Cover and transfer to a preheated oven at 350°F for 40 minutes, or until the chicken is cooked (the juices should run clear when pricked through the thickest part with a fork or skewer).

Put the cornstarch into a small cup or bowl, add ¼ cup water, and stir until loose. (This is called slaking.)

Remove the casserole from the heat, pour off the liquid into another saucepan, bring to a boil, and reduce to about 1¼ cups. Remove from the heat and let cool for 5 minutes. Put the egg yolks in a bowl, beat well, then beat in 1 tablespoon of the lemon juice. Beat the mixture into the sauce, a little at a time, and very slowly. Taste and adjust the seasoning. Add the remaining tablespoon of lemon juice if it needs a little more acidity. Reserve a tablespoon or so of the lemon zest and stir the remainder into the sauce.

Remove the chicken from the oven and pour the sauce over. Serve topped with chopped dill and the reserved lemon zest.

Butter is the cooking medium in the area of Italy with which this recipe is associated. It is traditionally served with *Risotto alla Milanese*—a most delicious concoction of saffron, arborio rice, white wine, chicken stock, and butter. Unquestionably, resist the temptation to cook this dish in olive oil.

Osso Buco

1¼ sticks butter

1 onion, chopped

1 carrot, chopped

2 celery stalks, chopped

3 garlic cloves, sliced

1¾ cups canned Italian tomatoes (14½ oz. can)

leaves from 2 sprigs of thyme

2 tablespoons chopped fresh flat-leaf parsley

2 bay leaves

½ cup peanut, canola, or safflower oil

⅔ cup all-purpose flour, seasoned with salt and pepper

4 large slices veal shank crosscuts, about 2 inches thick, 10 oz. each

1 cup white wine

2 cups chicken stock (page 134)

salt and freshly ground black pepper

SERVES 4

Heat the butter in a large skillet, add the onion, carrot, celery, and garlic, and cook gently until softened and translucent—take care not to burn the butter. Add the tomatoes and herbs and simmer for 10 minutes to make a sauce. Transfer to a casserole and set aside. Add the oil to the skillet and heat gently.

Put the flour, salt, and pepper in a plastic bag, add the veal, and shake to coat. Add to the skillet and sauté until browned on all sides. Transfer to the casserole.

To deglaze the skillet, add the wine, bring to a boil, and reduce to 2 tablespoons. Add the stock and scrape up any sediment from the base of the pan, so as not to lose any flavor. Bring to a boil, season with salt and pepper, then transfer to the casserole. The liquid should nearly cover the meat; if not, top up with boiling water.

Cover tightly with a lid and cook in a preheated oven at 325°F for about 1½ hours, checking the liquid from time to time to see that the meat is not drying out. When the meat is tender, lift it onto a serving dish and check that the sauce is of a coating consistency. If it is too thin, transfer to the top of the stove and simmer until reduced. There should be about 3 cups. Pour it over the meat and serve with *Risotto alla Milanese* or mashed potatoes.

Risotto alla Milanese Put a large pinch of saffron threads into a bowl, pour over ½ cup boiling water, and let soak for 30 minutes. Put 4 cups rich chicken stock in a saucepan, bring to a boil, then add the saffron and its soaking liquid. Melt 1 stick butter in a large saucepan, add 1 finely chopped onion, and sauté very gently for 5 minutes until softened but not browned. Add 2½ cups superfino arborio risotto rice and sauté gently until it whitens, about 5 minutes. Add 1 cup dry white wine and let it bubble away to about 1 teaspoon. Add a ladle of the stock and simmer until absorbed. Continue adding stock, a ladle at a time, until all the stock has been used and the rice is still al dente. Stir in 2 cups grated Parmesan cheese and serve with the Osso Buco.

Daubes are dishes in which the meat is sealed in a lidded casserole and simmered in wine for a long time and is so soft that it can be cut with a spoon. The wine used here is a white one, which is rather unexpected with beef. It gives a more acid pungency to the dish and goes well with olives.

Provençal Daube of Beef

2 tablespoons olive oil

2 large onions, about 1 lb., sliced

2 lb. beef boneless rib-eye roast, trimmed and tied

2 garlic cloves, sliced

2 tomatoes, chopped

1 carrot, sliced crosswise

2 sprigs of thyme

2 fresh bay leaves

⅔ cup white wine

6 green olives, pitted

6 black olives, pitted

salt and freshly ground black pepper

SERVES 4

Heat the oil in a large skillet, add the onions, and sauté until softened but not browned. Transfer to a casserole just big enough to hold the beef.

Add the rib-eye roast to the skillet, brown it on all sides, then transfer to the casserole.

Add the garlic, tomatoes, carrot, thyme, and bay leaves to the skillet and mix well. Sauté until lightly browned, then pack the mixture around the beef in the casserole.

Pour the wine into the skillet, scraping any brown bits into the liquid. Season with salt and pepper and pour the mixture over the beef. Cover with a lid, transfer to a preheated oven at 300°F, and cook for 3 hours until all the liquid has been absorbed. If necessary, take the lid off for the last 40 minutes to reduce the excess liquid.

Add the olives to the casserole, heat through for 5 minutes, then serve the daube with lots of creamy mashed potatoes and a few baby carrots—the beef should by now be so tender that it falls to pieces when touched.

Irish Carbonnade

Carbonnades are native to Belgium and northern France, where they are always flavored with beer. I find good Irish stout much superior. A carbonnade uses caramelized sugar to sweeten the gravy. In this version, stout gives an extra touch of bitterness and this must be corrected to be pleasing. Lots of sweet shallots or pickling onions will also add to the sweetness.

2 tablespoons duck or goose fat, or peanut, canola, or safflower oil

1½ lb. flank steak, cut into 1-inch cubes

3 tablespoons sugar

1 onion, chopped

2 tablespoons all-purpose flour

12 shallots

2 cups hot beef stock (page 136)

1½ cups stout, such as Guinness

2 tablespoons red wine vinegar

3 cloves

2 bay leaves

salt and freshly ground black pepper

SERVES 4

Heat the fat or oil in a large skillet. Season the meat with salt and pepper, add to the skillet, and sauté until browned on all sides. Transfer to a large, flameproof casserole.

Add the sugar to the skillet and let it cook until it becomes a good chestnut color. Add the onion, flour, and shallots and mix well for about 30 seconds. Stir in the stock and stout, bring to a boil, and cook for 1 minute. Add the vinegar, cloves, bay leaves, and a little more seasoning, then pour it all over the meat in the casserole. Mix well.

Cover the casserole and let simmer very gently on top of the stove or in a preheated oven at 325°F for 1½–2 hours. Remove from the heat or the oven and pour off the liquid into a separate saucepan or skillet. Bring to a boil and simmer to reduce the liquid to a coating consistency. Return it to the casserole and serve. Piles of creamy mashed potatoes and sautéed mushrooms would be suitable accompaniments.

Steak and Kidney Pudding

The richness of the gravy in a steak and kidney pudding is unique. It is produced by the meats giving all their juices to thicken and flavor the stock in the pudding without the liquid having come to a boil. Once the pudding has been broached, the gravy actually thickens even more and should be thinned down with more stock unless you like a very thick gravy. I know of no other dish that works like this, certainly not a steak and kidney pie. It is a very interesting example of casserole cooking and is classic British food at its best. Serve the pudding wrapped in a linen napkin, with a small pitcher of extra stock for thinning down the gravy.

Steak and Kidney Pudding

step-by-step

1 lb. beef kidney

¼ cup all-purpose flour

1 teaspoon salt

¼ teaspoon freshly ground black pepper

1½ lb. boneless shank crosscuts or chuck steak, cut into 1-inch cubes*

2 onions, chopped

1 garlic clove, crushed (optional)

2¾ cups beef stock (page 136) or water

SUET CRUST

3⅓ cups self-rising flour

1 teaspoon salt

2¼ cups suet** or shortening

1 heatproof ceramic bowl, 9-cup (2¼ quart) capacity

SERVES 4–6

*The cooking time will differ for different kinds of meat. In Step 10, chuck will take 4 hours, while shank will take 6 hours.

**Suet is often used in British pastry making, especially in savory dishes. It is hard white beef fat, usually from around the kidneys of the animal. Your butcher will be able to give you some. Chill until firm, dust with flour, then grate it on the large side of a box grater or in a food processor before using to make pastry. Though it may sound a strange ingredient, it famously makes the best pastry.

1 To make the suet crust, put the flour, salt, and suet or shortening into a bowl, add about 2¾ cups water, or enough to make a firm mixture. Mix to form a ball.

Reserve one-third of the dough to make the lid and transfer the remainder to a floured surface. Roll out to a disk 16 inches in diameter.

2 Cut out a wedge from the disk—this will allow it to fit the bowl easily. Use to line the bowl, letting it overlap the edges by 1 inch all round (trim back any excess). Stick any joins together with a little water.

6 Heat the stock, season to taste, then pour about half the stock over the meat to cover it. Reserve the remaining stock.

Roll out the remaining dough to make a disk just big enough to cover the top of the basin.

7 Fold the overlapping edges of the pastry inwards over the top of the meat and brush the top edge with water.

3 Cut the kidney into 1-inch chunks, discarding all the membrane. You will lose about a quarter of the weight.

4 Put the flour, salt, and pepper into a plastic bag, seal, and shake. Add the steak and kidney and, holding the neck of the bag lightly, shake it vigorously until all the meat is evenly coated with the seasoned flour.

5 Shake off any excess flour and transfer all the meat into the bowl. Sprinkle with the onion and garlic, if using, as you do so.

8 Put the lid of pastry on top of the basin and crimp the edges inside the rim to seal the pudding. Don't worry if a little stock escapes: it will be absorbed.

9 Fold a large sheet of foil to make a pleat down the middle to allow for expansion. Put on top of the basin and tie a length of kitchen twine firmly around the edge, under the lip of the basin. Tie a "handle" of kitchen twine from side to side, to make the pudding easier to lift in and out of the Dutch oven.

10 Lower into a Dutch oven, three-quarters fill it with boiling water, and cover with a lid. Return to a boil, reduce the heat, and let simmer for 4–6 hours, topping it up with boiling water from time to time.

Serve. After the first helping has been served, gently mix in the rest of the stock to thin the gravy for second helpings.

Serve a navarin when the new season's vegetables are being harvested and the lamb is just that little bit older. To give the gravy that rich color and sweet flavor, a little sugar is sprinkled either onto the lamb as it is browned, or into the pan, which makes it easier to control. It is then caramelized: the darker the sugar becomes, the less sweet the stew will be.

Navarin of Lamb

2 lb. boneless shoulder of lamb

1 tablespoon butter

1 tablespoon sugar

2 tablespoons all-purpose flour

2¾ cups lamb or beef stock (page 136)

4 tomatoes, peeled and seeded, or 1 cup canned Italian plum tomatoes (10 oz. can)

2 garlic cloves, crushed

1 teaspoon chopped fresh thyme leaves

1 sprig of rosemary

1 bay leaf

salt and freshly ground black pepper

SPRING VEGETABLES

8 new potatoes, scraped and cooked

8 baby carrots, scraped and cooked

8 baby white turnips, cooked

1 cup cooked green peas

1 cup green beans, cooked and cut into ½-inch strips

SERVES 4

Cut the lamb into 1-inch cubes, discarding any fat. Heat the butter in a heavy skillet. Season the lamb and sauté in 2 batches, browning the pieces evenly all over and draining them of fat as they are put aside onto a dish.

Reserve 3 tablespoons of the fat in the skillet and discard the rest. Sprinkle the sugar into the skillet and let caramelize to a deep golden brown. (Be careful not to caramelize it too much, as it burns easily.) Quickly mix in the flour, return the meat to the skillet, and mix well: this will let the flour cook a little.

Add the stock, then the tomatoes, garlic, and herbs. Stir gently and bring to a boil. Season to taste, then transfer to a lidded casserole, cover, and simmer in a preheated oven at 375°F for 40–50 minutes or until the meat is tender.

If there is too much liquid, strain it off into a saucepan, bring to a boil, and simmer until reduced to about 2¾ cups. Taste and adjust the seasoning, then add the cooked vegetables. Mix them gently through the liquid, then transfer them and the liquid to the casserole, stir gently, then reheat in the oven for about 10 minutes. Serve.

This is a very simple dish but surprisingly effective considering how few ingredients there are, so make sure you adjust the seasoning carefully as it makes such a difference. Ideally, each steak should be about 1 inch thick and weigh about 8 oz. Trim the stem end only of the okra, taking off the tiniest layer of the already-cut surface, to discourage the sticky liquid from oozing out.

Greek Braised Lamb with Okra

3 tablespoons olive oil

4 lamb steaks, about 2 lb., cut from the leg and deboned

1 small onion, sliced

2 garlic cloves, crushed

4 tomatoes, peeled and seeded

8 oz. okra, trimmed

salt and freshly ground black pepper

TO SERVE

new potatoes

chopped fresh flat-leaf parsley

SERVES 4

Heat the oil in a large, wide, shallow, flameproof casserole or saucepan. Season the meat with salt and pepper, add to the pan, and brown the pieces all over. Remove the meat with a slotted spoon, put on a plate, and set aside in a warm place.

Add the onion and garlic to the pan and cook until softened and lightly browned. Add the tomatoes and simmer to a pulp.

Return the lamb to the pan, turn to coat, taste and adjust the seasoning, and cover with a lid. Bring to a boil on top of the stove, then transfer to a preheated oven and simmer at 350°F for 20 minutes.

Add the okra, cover, and simmer for a further 20 minutes, removing the lid for the last 10 minutes of cooking time, to let the liquid reduce enough to just coat the meat without becoming oily. Serve with new potatoes and sprinkle with chopped parsley.

A picnic shoulder of pork is known as a "hand" of pork in Europe. It is much the best part, to my mind, for roasting or braising, as it has just the right amount of fat, whereas the leg is so lean as to make it difficult to keep moist. Anyway, a certain amount of fat is needed in this dish to moisten the beans—or perhaps it's the other way round and the beans are needed to mop up the juices. Either way, it makes for a scrumptious dinner.

Tuscan Pork and Bean Casserole

1½ cups dried cannellini beans or great Northern beans

¼ cup olive oil

12 oz. carrots, cut into 1-inch chunks

4 onions, peeled but left whole

4 small turnips

1 sprig of thyme

1 bay leaf

6 peppercorns

6 garlic cloves, or to taste

4 lb. fresh picnic shoulder of pork

8 oz. thick-cut bacon, cut into chunks

1½ lb. small potatoes, peeled

8 oz. fresh green beans

salt and freshly ground black pepper

SERVES 4

Put the dried beans in a bowl, cover with water, and let soak overnight. Drain, transfer the beans to a saucepan, cover with water again, and bring to a boil. Drain and discard this water, reserving the beans to add to the stew.

Heat the oil in a large ovenproof casserole with a lid, then stir in the carrots, onions, turnips, thyme, bay leaf, peppercorns, and garlic. Sauté gently until softened but not browned.

Meanwhile, cut the rind off the pork and reserve it. Add the pork, its rind, the bacon chunks, and the drained beans to the casserole. Cover with water, add salt and pepper, and bring to a boil on top of the stove. Transfer to a preheated oven and simmer at 325°F for 1½ hours, or until the beans are tender.

After 1 hour, taste and adjust the seasoning, then add the potatoes for the last 30 minutes and the fresh green beans for the last 5 minutes.

To serve, remove and discard the pork rind, lift the meat onto a dish, and carve into thick slices. Add the vegetables and beans to the dish and serve with a separate small pitcher of the cooking juices.

Try a *choucroute* at least once in your life and you'll be hooked. It reheats very well and doesn't mind waiting, so cook more than you need and have it twice. Jazz it up with duck confit or roast goose for a special treat (home-cooked or from a French gourmet store). Goose or duck fat is also sold by the jar in the same stores and adds considerably to the flavor. Butter is also good, but just don't use olive oil—it's completely the wrong flavor, from the wrong part of the world.

Choucroute Garnie

2 lb. bottled sauerkraut,
4 cups by volume

5 tablespoons goose fat or butter

8 oz. thick-cut bacon, cubed

1 carrot, sliced

1 onion, sliced

1 bay leaf

2 sprigs of thyme

6 peppercorns

½ cup white wine

2 cups chicken stock (page 134)

4 pork neck cutlets

8 frankfurters

salt and freshly ground black pepper

SERVES 4

Drain the sauerkraut, empty it into a large saucepan, and cover with water. Stir well, empty into a colander, then drain.

Heat 3 tablespoons of the the goose fat or butter in a large, flameproof casserole, add the bacon, carrot, onion, herbs, and peppercorns, and cook gently for 5 minutes. Add the wine, bring to a boil, and reduce by half.

Add the stock and stir in the drained sauerkraut. Cover with a lid, bring to a boil, and cook in a preheated oven at 325°F for 2 hours.

Meanwhile, heat the remaining goose fat or butter in a skillet, add the pork cutlets, season with salt and pepper, and sauté until browned. Tuck the pork cutlets into the sauerkraut for the last hour. Add the frankfurters for the final 5 minutes.

Note Choucroute is traditionally served on a large platter in the middle of the table. Since Alsace is its original home, a cold beer or a glass of spicy gewürztztraminer wine would be a suitable accompaniment.

Cassoulet de Toulouse

Cassoulets, the pride of many southern areas in France, are named after the region from which they come, *Cassoulet de Toulouse* being one of the most famous. They show off the local garlic sausages, while the beans also play an important part—some flageolets are the pale green variety, not very often found fresh outside the area. Luckily, all this doesn't affect the magnificence of the dish, which calls out for robust red wine and genial company. Don't worry if the dish has to wait. Just add a bit more hot stock or water to the pot and lower the oven temperature until ready to serve.

Cassoulet de Toulouse
step-by-step

2½ cups dried flageolet or haricot beans

8 oz. thick-cut hickory-smoked pork

1 stick butter or ½ cup olive oil or goose fat

1 lb. boneless shoulder of lamb, cubed

1 lb. pork neck meat, cubed

4 garlic cloves, crushed

2 tomatoes, peeled and chopped

2 sprigs of thyme

2 sprigs of marjoram, or ½ teaspoon dried

2¾ cups beef stock (page 136)

8 oz. whole piece of garlic sausage,
cut into bite-size pieces

¼ cup fresh breadcrumbs

salt and freshly ground black pepper

SERVES 6

1 Put the beans in a bowl, cover with cold water, and let soak for at least 8 hours, but preferably overnight. Next day, drain them, put in a large, flameproof casserole, cover with fresh water, bring to a boil on top of the stove, then drain again. Cover with cold water for a third time.

2 Add the hickory-smoked pork, bring to a boil, reduce the heat, and simmer for about 30 minutes, being careful not to let the beans start to disintegrate.

6 Strain the beans into a bowl, reserving their liquid. Spread some of the beans in a thick layer in the bottom of a deep casserole dish.

7 Add a layer of meat, another layer of sausage, and a layer of beans. Repeat until all have been used up, finishing with a layer of beans.

3 Meanwhile, heat 2 tablespoons of the butter, oil, or goose fat in a large skillet, add the lamb and pork pieces in batches, and sauté until lightly brown, adding extra butter, oil, or fat as necessary. Do not crowd the skillet and remove the meat to a plate between batches. (They are cooked in batches so that they sauté, rather than boiling in their own juices.)

4 Return all the meat to the skillet, add the garlic, tomatoes, herbs, salt, and pepper. Cook for 1–2 minutes, or until the tomatoes soften to a purée.

Add enough beef stock to cover, bring to a boil, and simmer for 40 minutes, or until the meat is tender and the gravy is well reduced and concentrated.

5 Remove the pork from the beans, transfer to a cutting board, and cut into bite-size pieces.

8 Add the meat cooking liquid, then the reserved bean liquid, filling the casserole almost to the top.

9 Heat 3 tablespoons of the butter, olive oil, or goose fat in a skillet, add the breadcrumbs, and sauté until golden brown. Remove from the heat, then drain.

10 Sprinkle the crumbs over the top of the cassoulet, then cook in a preheated oven at 350°F for about 1½ hours until crusty. Serve with a green salad and plenty of red wine.

A traditional hotpot was an earthenware vessel with a tight-fitting lid, tall enough to take mutton cutlets standing upright, so it was very tall! Nowadays, any casserole will do, as the name refers to the contents rather than the pot. The Lancashire version is always topped with a lid of sliced or chunked potatoes and usually contains beef as well as lamb. This recipe is just one of several local variations; other hotpots can include liver and bacon, or fish, usually pilchards. When times were hard, just vegetables fried in fat would be used.

Lancashire Hotpot

1 lb. beef for stew, trimmed of fat

8 oz. shoulder of lamb, trimmed of fat

2 lamb's kidneys, cleaned and trimmed (optional)

1 tablespoon all-purpose flour

2 tablespoons beef drippings or butter (optional)

1 onion, thinly sliced

1 carrot, cut into chunks

1 bay leaf

1¼ cups beef stock (page 136) or water

½ teaspoon salt

1 teaspoon sugar

¼ teaspoon freshly ground black pepper

1 teaspoon anchovy paste

12 oz. potatoes, cut into walnut-size chunks

SERVES 4

Cut the meats into 1-inch pieces and sprinkle with the flour. Mix well, then shake off the excess flour through a large strainer. Arrange the meats in a flameproof casserole. If preferred, heat the drippings or butter in a skillet, add the vegetables, and sauté until lightly browned. Transfer the vegetables, whether browned or not, to the casserole. Add the bay leaf, season the boiling stock or water with the salt, sugar, pepper, and anchovy paste, then pour over the meats.

Cover, bring to a boil on top of the stove, then transfer to a preheated oven at 350°F and simmer for 1 hour.

Arrange the potatoes, rounded side up, on top of the meats and spoon some of the meat juices over the top to glaze. Cover and return the casserole to the oven for a further hour. Remove the lid to allow the potatoes to become lightly browned and, increasing the heat if necessary, cook for a further 30 minutes.

A "tian" is a shallow clay dish in the language of Provence and also any dish cooked in it. Overlapping layers of vegetables are arranged in the dish, then baked in the oven. Some vegetables, such as tomatoes and zucchini, are prone to throwing off a lot of liquid, so it's a good idea to remove some beforehand by roasting or salting (rather inelegantly known as "degorging").

Provençal Tian

6 large ripe tomatoes, halved

4 garlic cloves, finely sliced

6 small eggplants, thickly sliced lengthwise

3 zucchini or yellow squash, thickly sliced lengthwise

⅓ cup olive oil, plus extra for brushing

2 large red onions, thickly sliced

2 tablespoons chopped fresh thyme leaves

salt and freshly ground black pepper

TOPPING

grated zest of 1 lemon

3 garlic cloves, crushed

about 1 cup dried breadcrumbs

½ cup freshly grated Parmesan cheese

sprigs of basil, to serve (optional)

SERVES 4–6

Put the tomatoes on a baking sheet, cut side up, and push slivers of garlic into each one. Roast in a preheated oven at 400°F for about 30 minutes to remove some of the moisture.

Put the sliced eggplants and squash on a plate, sprinkle with salt, and set aside for 30 minutes to extract some of the moisture. Rinse and pat dry with paper towels.

Heat the oil in a large skillet, add the onions, and sauté until softened and translucent. Remove from the skillet and spread over the base of a tian or other shallow ceramic ovenproof dish.

Arrange overlapping layers of the tomatoes, eggplants, and squash on top—arrange them in lines across the dish, like fish scales. Tuck the chopped thyme between the layers.

Brush with the extra olive oil and cook in a preheated oven at 400°F for about 20 minutes.

Meanwhile, to make the topping, grate the lemon zest into a bowl, add the crushed garlic, and mix well. Stir in the breadcrumbs and cheese, then sprinkle over the top of the tian. Continue cooking for at least 30 minutes or until browned, finishing under the broiler if necessary. Serve topped with basil leaves, if using.

The Moroccan tagine is one of the world's archetypal casseroles, both as a recipe and as a cooking pot. Made of glazed earthenware, this pot with a conical lid is placed over a brazier of hot coals—you see food stalls in the souks with small individual brazier-tagine combos bubbling all morning in preparation for the lunchtime onslaught. Traditionally, the only ovens are owned by bakers and used by householders to cook homemade bread and not, as is the custom in Italy, to simmer stews or slow-roasted meats.

Just as many food words in the countries ranging from Northern India to the Middle East and North Africa seem to have similar origins, so, too, many of the regional dishes have similar themes. Some authorities claim that Persia (now Iran) was the wellspring for some of the best-known dishes of the region, while others regard Turkey as more influential. Certainly, there is a common theme from Morocco to North India (the Indian lamb dish on page 95 is a recognizable relation of the Persian lamb on page 80 or the Turkish lamb on page 82).

Lamb, chicken, and game appear most often in casseroles—because the whole region is predominantly Muslim, there are no pork dishes and not much beef. Above all, there is a delicious variety of vegetables and interesting ways of cooking them—as side dishes, pickles, and in casseroles with rice or couscous.

The use of nuts and dried fruits, plus spices such as saffron and cinnamon, to flavor casseroles is one of the indications of Arab or Persian influence in cooking, wherever it appears.

AFRICA
AND THE
MIDDLE EAST

Chicken Tagine
with Quinces and Preserved Lemons

A tagine is the Moroccan clay cooking pot with a conical lid, and also any dish cooked in it. The shape encourages steam to rise into the lid, then drop back onto the meat, keeping it moist. Tagines often include fruits of various kinds, but the elegant, scented quince is a favorite in Morocco in the Fall. When unavailable, slightly unripe pears can be used instead, as they belong to the same botanical family. Preserved lemons add a salty tang: buy them in Middle Eastern food stores or make your own.

1 teaspoon ground saffron

1 inch fresh ginger, peeled and grated, or 1 teaspoon ground ginger

1½ tablespoons paprika

1 teaspoon freshly ground black pepper

2 teaspoons ground cinnamon

1 chicken, cut into 8 pieces

½ cup olive oil

2 large onions, grated

a pinch of saffron threads, soaked in boiling water for 30 minutes

6 garlic cloves, crushed

2 cinnamon sticks, broken in half

6 cloves

10 cardamom pods, lightly crushed

2 quinces, cored and cut into wedges

2 preserved lemons (optional)

cilantro leaves, to serve

SERVES 4

Put the ground saffron, ginger, paprika, pepper, and ground cinnamon into a bowl and mix well. Rub the chicken pieces in the mixture, put in a bowl, cover with plastic wrap, and marinate for at least 30 minutes or overnight in the refrigerator.

Heat the olive oil in a heavy, flameproof casserole. Add the chicken and sauté on all sides until golden. Add the onion, then the saffron threads and their soaking liquid, the garlic, cinnamon sticks, cloves, and cardamom pods. Add ½ cup water and bring to a boil on top of the stove. Cover and simmer on top of the stove or in a preheated oven at 300°F for 45 minutes, or until partially cooked.

Peel the quince wedges, add to the tagine, and continue cooking for another 30 minutes or until the chicken is done and the quinces are tender.

If using preserved lemons, cut them in quarters and scrape off and discard the flesh. Cut the peel into thick slices lengthwise and stir into the tagine. Heat for about 5-10 minutes, then serve the tagine sprinkled with cilantro leaves.

Cornish Hens
stuffed with Saffron Couscous

Although the couscous in this recipe is designed to be used as a stuffing, it is also delicious eaten on its own as a light lunch dish—albeit a shade sweet for the average tooth. The couscous sold in packages in the supermarket is precooked, so it only needs the correct amount of boiling water to be added to make it swell and yet stay fluffy when tossed with a fork. Too much water is disastrous and turns the mixture into a wet porridge. The delicious dried fruits and nuts used in the stuffing are typical of Muslim cooking and are found from Morocco to North India.

Cornish Hens
stuffed with Saffron Couscous

step-by-step

a large pinch of saffron threads

1 onion, chopped

¼ teaspoon white pepper

3 tablespoons butter

1 cinnamon stick

4 Cornish hens or 2 medium chickens

1 teaspoon honey

1 teaspoon ground cinnamon

salt

SAFFRON COUSCOUS STUFFING

6 tablespoons butter

1 cup quick-cook couscous

1 teaspoon salt

2 tablespoons orange flower water or a long curl of tangerine zest

⅔ cup seedless raisins

½ cup chopped almonds

2½ tablespoons sugar

2 teaspoons ground cinnamon

SERVES 4

1 To make the stuffing, heat half the butter in a large skillet, then add the couscous and salt. Pour on 1½ cups water, cover, and bring to a boil.

2 Set aside for about 10 minutes, or until well puffed up, then fluff with a fork to separate the grains.

5 Put the saffron, onion, pepper, butter, and cinnamon stick into a large, flameproof casserole, add 1 cup water, and bring to a boil. Simmer for 2 minutes.

6 Lightly sprinkle the Cornish hens inside and out with salt, then divide the stuffing into 4 portions and use to fill the cavities, packing it in very firmly.

3 Put the orange flower water in a saucepan, add the raisins, and bring to a boil. Turn off the heat and set aside to absorb the liquid. If using tangerine zest instead, add 2 tablespoons water as well.

4 Put the almonds into a dry skillet and toast over medium heat until golden.

5 Transfer the almonds to the couscous, then stir in the raisins, sugar, ground cinnamon, and the remaining butter.

7 Truss the birds with kitchen twine to keep the stuffing in place.

8 Stand the Cornish hens close together in the casserole, breasts down, spooning some of the saffron mixture over the top. Bring to a boil, cover, and simmer for 20 minutes, then turn them onto their sides and simmer for a further 20 minutes. Repeat this for a third time.

9 Prick the thighs with a fork—the juices should run clear. If not, cook for a further 10–20 minutes. When done, discard the twine and put the birds on a serving platter. Add the honey and ground cinnamon to the juices in the casserole, bring to a boil to make a thickish gravy, then pour over the birds and serve.

Persian Lamb Khoresh
with Saffron Chelo Rice

The rice needs a bit of practice to get it right, with a crust on the bottom (called *tak dip*), but not to have it burnt irrevocably onto the bottom of the pan. Try cheating with a nonstick one.

2 eggplants, peeled and quartered lengthwise

1 tablespoon salt

¾ cup clarified butter (see recipe introduction page 83)

3 onions, finely sliced

2 lb. boneless lamb, such as shoulder, cut into 1-inch cubes

1 teaspoon ground turmeric

½ teaspoon crushed black pepper

4 tomatoes, peeled and seeded

2 cups spinach

2 cups dried fruits, such as pitted dates, dried apricots, dried apples, or figs, chopped if large

freshly squeezed juice of 1 lime, plus lime wedges, to serve

salt and freshly ground black pepper

SAFFRON CHELO RICE

2½ cups basmati rice

½ teaspoon salt

1¼ sticks butter

a large pinch of saffron threads

SERVES 4

Sprinkle the eggplant wedges with the salt and set aside for 2 hours to draw out some of the liquid. Rinse well to remove the salt and pat dry with paper towels.

Heat the clarified butter in a flameproof casserole, add the eggplant quarters, and sauté until thoroughly browned on all sides. Remove with a slotted spoon, put on a plate, and keep them warm.

Add the onions to the casserole and sauté gently until softened and browned. Remove with a slotted spoon and add to the plate of eggplants.

Add a little more butter if necessary, then add the lamb cubes and sprinkle with the turmeric and pepper. Sauté, turning the pieces, until browned on all sides.

Return the onions to the pan, then add the tomatoes. Add water to cover and salt and pepper to taste. Bring to a boil, reduce the heat, and simmer gently for 30 minutes, or until the lamb is half-cooked. Add the eggplants, spinach, and dried fruits. Continue simmering for 30 minutes, or until the lamb is tender. Taste and adjust the seasoning with a little lime juice. Serve with the Chelo Rice and lime wedges.

Saffron Chelo Rice

Put the rice in a bowl, cover with plenty of cold water, and soak for at least 2 hours, or overnight. Drain well.

Fill a large saucepan with water, add the salt, bring to a boil, and trickle in the rice slowly so that the water never stops boiling. Cook for 10 minutes. Drain.

Put the butter in a skillet with lid, add 2 cups water, and heat until the butter has melted. Pour off half the butter water into a measuring cup. Add the rice to the skillet and cook quickly, so that it sticks to the base of the pan, about 1 minute. Add the rest of the butter water and the saffron threads, cover the skillet, and cook over a very gentle heat for about 30 minutes, or until all the water has been absorbed and the base has dried out again.

Serve from the skillet or turn it out onto a platter: the crisp, slightly burnt rice from the bottom of the pan is highly prized.

Note Like most casseroles, this one is delicious cooled and chilled. The following day, crack any fat off the top and discard it, then reheat the lamb before serving (page 142).

Turkish Lamb
with Butternut Squash and Zucchini

Turkey, like Iran, loves butter—soup, for instance is often topped with butter melted with paprika. For cooking, the butter should be clarified, so the milky residue is drained out so that it cannot burn and taint the dish. The easiest way to clarify butter is to cut the sticks into slices, put into a bowl, cover with plastic wrap, and microwave on HIGH for 1½ minutes. Let it settle for 2 minutes, then pour off the clear oil and discard the residue. Store in the refrigerator.

2 teaspoons ground cinnamon

2 teaspoons paprika

2 garlic cloves, crushed

1 teaspoon virgin olive oil

2 lb. lamb shoulder, cubed

1¼ cups clarified butter
(see recipe introduction)

2 onions, sliced

1 eggplant, peeled and sliced

1 red bell pepper, seeded
and cut into 8 strips

1 yellow or orange bell pepper,
seeded and cut into 8 strips

4 tomatoes, peeled,
halved, and seeded

½ butternut squash, peeled
and cut into ½-inch cubes

1 lb. baby new potatoes, about 20

4 oz. green beans, topped and tailed

a handful of okra, minimally
trimmed at the stalk end

2 medium zucchini,
cut into thick chunks

salt and freshly ground black pepper

SERVES 4

Put the cinnamon, paprika, garlic, and oil in a small bowl, mix well, then rub the meat with the paste. Let marinate in the refrigerator for about 30 minutes while you prepare the vegetables.

Heat the clarified butter in a flameproof casserole, add the onion, and sauté until softened and browned. Remove the onion from the casserole, add the meat, and sauté until browned on all sides, about 10 minutes. Return the onion to the pan.

Add enough water to cover and season with plenty of salt and pepper. Bring to a boil, reduce the heat and simmer for 40 minutes, until the meat begins to tenderize.

Tuck in the eggplant, bell peppers, tomatoes, butternut cubes, and potatoes, adding more water if necessary.

Taste and adjust the seasoning if necessary, cover with a lid, bring to a boil, then transfer to a preheated oven and simmer at 325°F until vegetables and meat are tender, about 40 minutes. Add the green beans, okra, and zucchini for the last 10 minutes of cooking.

The colors in this casserole are only equaled by its flavor. Both are startling and gorgeous. Don't overdo the harissa—just a little will just wake you up. Let the vegetables char and acquire a bit of barbecue flavor—and don't forget the yogurt.

North African Charred Vegetables

3 red onions, cut into wedges

18 cherry tomatoes

1 large zucchini, cut into wedges

6 oz. small red potatoes, halved

2 red bell peppers, seeded and cut into strips or wedges

1 yellow bell pepper, seeded and cut into strips or wedges

2 fennel bulbs, cut in wedges

⅓ cup olive oil

6 garlic cloves, crushed to a paste

½ teaspoon harissa paste

1 teaspoon ground cumin

1 tablespoon vinegar

1 tablespoon chopped fresh mint

1 tablespoon chopped fresh cilantro

2 teaspoons salt

2 cups thick plain yogurt, to serve

SERVES 4–6

Reserve 1 onion and 4 cherry tomatoes. Arrange the remaining vegetables in a roasting pan, drizzle with ¼ cup of the oil, and roast in a preheated oven at 475°F or the highest temperature available on your stove until they begin to char, about 30 minutes.

Lower the heat to 350°F. Remove the vegetables from the oven and transfer to a shallow casserole dish.

Put the crushed garlic in a small bowl and mash in the harissa, cumin, and remaining oil. Stir in the vinegar, mint, and cilantro. Mix this in with the vegetables, tuck in the last onion and 4 cherry tomatoes, sprinkle generously with salt, and return the casserole to the oven to bake for a further 25 minutes.

If there is too much liquid, pour it off into a small saucepan, bring to a boil, and simmer until reduced and concentrated in flavor. Pour back into the casserole. Serve with yogurt.

Is curry a casserole? In India there's no such thing as "curry" or "curry powder." What we think of as curry comes in countless different varieties, from stir-fries to casseroles, according to region, community, or religion. Curry powder was invented for British ex-patriates, who returned home to find that they missed the gorgeous spice mixes or masalas of the East, but it is a pale, flavorless imitation of the real thing.

The making of a masala is a very skilled business: every bride is given a spice box or *masala dani,* from which she blends her own mixtures into an infinite variety of flavors, different for each dish, and carefully handed down from mother to daughter.

The masala spices and flavorings are pounded, blended, and made into a paste or powder, then toasted to mature their flavors and release their oils before the next stage of cooking. In many dishes, the next step is to add ghee or oil, then the "trinity" of onion, garlic, and fresh ginger. Meat, poultry, or vegetables are added and simmered until done. Dishes are often then "tempered"—topped with a spicy fried onion mixture—before serving.

Most foods are cooked over direct heat, such as hot coals or an open stove. Closed ovens are not usual in domestic kitchens in this part of the world. However, in larger establishments, such as royal kitchens or big hotels, methods closer to oven-cooking of casseroles are sometimes seen. For instance, in the *dum pukht* cooking from the northern city of Lucknow, the spiced dish is transferred to a lidded pot and the whole is sealed with a rim of dough and allowed to cook gently in its own steam and juices, rather like a French daube.

INDIA

Fish Mollee

A *mollee* is a South Indian sauce, one of those dishes known wrongly in the rest of the world as a "curry." It is mostly used for poaching fish, but is also delicious as a medium for reheating cooked meats or vegetables. The first step is to make the sauce: after that, you may add what you like. In the south, this is often served with great mounds of fluffy rice flavored with cumin seed. In India, dishes such as this are cooked in the Indian wok, called a *karahi*.

1 lb. firm fish such as salmon, monkfish, or cod

1 tablespoon ground turmeric

1 teaspoon salt

⅓ cup ghee (clarified butter), butter, canola, or safflower oil

1 onion, chopped

1 garlic clove, crushed

2 small fresh green chiles, seeded if preferred, then chopped

1 inch fresh ginger, peeled and grated

12 cardamom pods, crushed

6 cloves, crushed

1 cinnamon stick, about 2 inches

2 cups canned coconut milk

freshly squeezed lemon juice, to taste

torn fresh cilantro leaves, to serve

SERVES 4

Cut the fish into 1-inch strips. Mix the turmeric and salt on a plate, roll the fish in the mixture, and set aside for a few minutes.

Meanwhile, heat the ghee, butter, or oil in a flameproof casserole or large saucepan. Add the onion, garlic, chiles, ginger, cardamom, cloves, and cinnamon stick and sauté until the onion is softened and translucent.

Add the coconut milk, heat until simmering, and cook until the mixture is quite thick. Add the fish to the casserole, then spoon the sauce over the top, making sure the fish is well covered. Cook for 10 minutes on top of the stove or in a preheated oven at 300°F, until the fish is opaque all the way through. Serve sprinkled with lemon juice and cilantro.

Kerala, on the southwest coast of India, is coconut country—and one of the great spice producing areas of the world (it was famous as such even in ancient times). It has a marvelous tradition of vegetarian cooking and an inspired touch with seafood.

Kerala Coconut Chile Shrimp

2 cups spinach, well washed

1 cup green beans

3 tablespoons ghee or peanut oil

2 onions, chopped

3 garlic cloves, chopped

1 inch fresh ginger, peeled and chopped

2 green chiles, seeded and chopped

1 tablespoon ground cumin

1 teaspoon freshly ground black pepper

6 green cardamom pods, crushed

2 cloves

a pinch of salt

freshly squeezed juice of ½ lemon

2 cups thick coconut milk

1 lb. peeled, uncooked shrimp

3 tablespoons chopped fresh cilantro

TO SERVE (OPTIONAL)

3–4 green chiles, sliced

a handful of cilantro leaves

SERVES 4

Bring a large saucepan of water to a boil and plunge in the spinach for 20 seconds. Remove with a slotted spoon and refresh under cold running water to stop the cooking process; squeeze out as much water as possible. Set aside. Add the beans and cook just until crunchy, about 3 minutes. Drain, refresh in cold water, drain again, and add to the spinach.

Heat the ghee or oil in an ovenproof casserole, add the onion, garlic, ginger, and chiles, and sauté until soft. Add the cumin, pepper, cardamom, cloves, salt, and 1 teaspoon of the lemon juice and cook for 5 minutes.

Stir in the coconut milk. Add the beans and shrimp, then stir in the chopped cilantro and the rest of the lemon juice. Cook in a preheated oven at 300°F for about 25 minutes, or until the shrimp have just become opaque. Add the spinach for the last 5 minutes to reheat. Do not overcook or the shrimp will be tough and tasteless.

Sprinkle with the sliced green chiles and a handful of cilantro leaves, then serve with plain rice or rice mixed with pan-toasted cumin seeds.

Saffron and Pistachio Biryani

The biryani is a Muslim dish, often linked with the "gourmet" city of Hyderabad, and especially popular in North India and Pakistan. It often includes chicken or lamb, but a vegetarian version is also delicious. For celebrations, it may have gold or silver leaf on top.

a large pinch of saffron threads

2½ teaspoons salt

1 cup butter ghee (clarified butter)

2¾ cups basmati rice

2 cinnamon sticks

6 cloves

2 bay leaves

6 green cardamom pods, crushed

1 tablespoon ground cumin

½ onion, sliced

1 inch fresh ginger, peeled and sliced

2 red chiles, seeded and sliced

3 garlic cloves, crushed

4 chicken breasts, skinless and boneless

1 cup plain whole-milk yogurt

1 tablespoon chopped fresh mint

1 tablespoon lightly chopped cilantro

TO SERVE

½ onion, fried till crisp, then crumbled

½ cup green pistachio nuts, shelled, blanched and peeled

⅓ cup almonds, toasted in a dry skillet, then sliced

⅓ cup raisins, soaked in 2 tablespoons boiling water for 30 minutes

a handful of cilantro leaves

SERVES 4

Put the saffron into a large saucepan with ⅔ cup water and ½ teaspoon of the salt. Bring to a boil, then set aside to cool.

Melt 6 tablespoons of the ghee in a second saucepan. Add the rice and sauté gently, stirring continuously, until the rice is white and opaque, about 5 minutes. Add 4 cups water, 1 cinnamon stick, 3 cloves, 1 bay leaf, 1 teaspoon salt, and half the cardamom. Cover with a lid, bring to a boil, reduce the heat, and simmer until all the water has been absorbed, about 10–15 minutes. (The rice will be slightly undercooked.)

Measure 2⅔ cups of this partially cooked rice and add to the pan of saffron water. Stir well, cover with a lid, bring to a boil, and cook for a couple of minutes or until the rice has absorbed all the water.

Add ½ cup water to the remaining white rice, stir, cover, bring to a boil, and cook for a couple of minutes or until the rice has absorbed all the water.

Measure a further 2⅔ cups of this rice and mix it gently with the saffron rice to give a yellow and white mixture.

Spread the remaining white rice into an a shallow casserole dish and set aside.

Rinse out the saucepan, add the remaining ghee and heat gently. Stir in the remaining cardamom, cloves, cinnamon stick, bay leaf, and the ground cumin and sauté to release the spice aroma.

Meanwhile, put the onion, ginger, chiles, garlic, and 5 tablespoons water in a blender and purée until smooth. Pour this mixture into the pan of hot spices and heat until the water has boiled away and the ghee begins to sauté the mixture.

Add the chicken and seal all over without browning it or the spices. Add the yogurt, mint, cilantro, and remaining salt and cover with a lid. Raise the heat and simmer, without boiling, for 20 minutes. (Don't worry when the sauce appears to split and become buttery.)

Remove the chicken and arrange on top of the rice in the casserole, pour the yogurt sauce over, cover, and cook in a preheated oven at 375°F for about 20 minutes while the rice absorbs the liquid.

Remove from the oven and arrange the bi-colored rice on top. Return to the oven for 5 minutes to heat through. Top with the onion, nuts, raisins, and cilantro and serve.

Spiced Lamb
with Coconut

A gentle casserole "curry" with plenty of flavor, especially if you can marinate it overnight. The recipe comes from Gujerat, one of the northwestern states of India, and it shows several typical methods of cooking casserole dishes. The Indian flavor "trinity" of onions, garlic, and ginger is stir-fried first, then a subtle combination of traditional spices is added and partially cooked to release their aromas. After the pieces of lamb have been added and cooked to tenderness, the dish is finished with a final "tempering" of stir-fried onions and mustard seeds. Compare it with the lamb dishes in the Middle East chapter and you will notice how they are related. Serve the lamb with other Indian dishes, such as one of the spicy vegetable dishes (page 98), a dhaal (lentils), a chutney, and rice or naan bread.

This recipe may also be adapted to the *dum pukht* cooking method originating in the royal kitchens of Lucknow, in the Central Indian state of Uttar Pradesh. At the end of cooking time, the dish is transferred to a lidded casserole, sealed with a ring of dough (or a sheet of foil), like a French daube, and steamed for 15 minutes.

Spiced Lamb
with Coconut

step-by-step

2 lb. leg or shoulder of lamb,
boned and cubed

3 cups canned coconut milk

a handful of fresh coconut slivers
or 1 tablespoon unsweetened dried shredded
coconut, pan-toasted

a handful of cilantro, fresh methi (fenugreek),
or curry leaves, to serve

TEMPERING

2 tablespoons mustard oil or peanut oil

2 red onions, cut into wedges

2 tablespoons mustard seeds

SPICY MASALA PASTE

⅓ cup peanut oil

3 onions, chopped

2 inches fresh ginger, peeled and grated

3 large garlic cloves, chopped

1 teaspoon ground cinnamon

1 tablespoon ground cumin

1 tablespoon ground coriander

¼ teaspoon ground cardamom

1 teaspoon ground turmeric

2 teaspoons hot red pepper flakes

3 tablespoons vinegar

1 teaspoon salt

SERVES 4

1 To make the masala paste, heat the oil
in a karahi (wok), skillet, or metal
casserole dish, add the onions, ginger,
and garlic, and stir-fry until lightly browned.

2 Add the cinnamon, cumin, ground
coriander, cardamom, turmeric, and
pepper flakes and cook until the fragrance
is released, about 3–4 minutes.

Variation

Lamb Dum Pukht Follow the main recipe, using yogurt instead of coconut milk, to
step 5. For the last 10 minutes of cooking time, transfer the contents of the pan to a
lidded casserole dish. Make a simple dough of flour and water and roll out to a 1-inch
thick sausage, long enough to fit around the rim of your casserole. Press the dough on
top of the rim, then press the lid on top to make a tight seal. Alternatively, press a sheet
of aluminum foil on top, then put on the lid. Cook in a preheated oven at 400°F for
about 15 minutes. Break open the seal at the table—the aroma is wonderful.

3 Stir in the vinegar and salt.

4 Add the lamb to the pan and sauté, turning frequently, for about 10 minutes until lightly browned on all sides. At this point, you may remove it from the heat, let cool, then chill overnight to marinate and develop the flavors (if time is short, this step may be omitted).

5 Add about 2⅔ cups of the coconut milk. Add water to cover, heat to simmering, then cook until the meat is tender, about 40 minutes. Stir from time to time to prevent the mixture from sticking to the pan. Stir in the rest of the coconut milk and cook for a further 10 minutes.

6 Meanwhile, put the coconut in a dry karahi or skillet and stir-fry for a few minutes until lightly golden: take care, the pieces can easily burn. Set aside.

7 To make the tempering, heat the oil in a karahi or skillet, add the onion and mustard seeds, and stir-fry until the onion is softened and dark golden brown around the edges. Remove from the heat.

8 Transfer the lamb to a serving dish, spoon the tempering over the top, and the coconut on top of that. Add the cilantro, fresh methi, or curry leaves, if using, and serve with other Indian dishes.

Dum Aloo
Steamed Spicy Potatoes

This is Indian comfort food: I could eat it by the bucketful. *Dum* means "steam" and *aloo* means "potatoes" in this steam-fry method of Indian casserole cooking. It is usually served with a number of other dishes: a dhaal (lentil), perhaps three chutneys—one sweet, one spicy, and one sour—plus rice (in the south) or naan bread (in the north). It is also rolled up in the delicious crispy pancake called a dosa to form a masala dosa. But this dish doesn't have to be Indian: serve it with any meat or poultry dishes.

1 lb. baby potatoes or medium ones cut into chunks

2 tablespoons shelled green peas (optional)

3 tablespoons ghee or peanut oil (never olive oil)

1 onion, chopped

2 garlic cloves, crushed

1 inch fresh ginger, peeled and grated

1 tablespoon ground cumin

1 tablespoon ground coriander or 2 tablespoons coriander seeds, crushed

2 teaspoons hot red pepper flakes, or 2 fresh chiles, seeded if preferred, then chopped

2 tomatoes, peeled, halved, and seeded

1 cup spinach (optional)

salt, to taste

SERVES 4

Cook the potatoes in boiling salted water until partially cooked. Drain. Cook the peas, if using, in the same way.

Heat the ghee or oil in a lidded casserole dish, add the onion, garlic, and ginger and stir-fry until golden brown. Add the salt and spices and cook until they become aromatic, about 5 minutes.

Add the tomatoes, bring to a boil, reduce the heat, then simmer to a purée. Add the potatoes, mix gently to cover with the onion mixture, then cover with a lid and simmer until done, about 20 minutes. If using peas or spinach, add them for the last 2–3 minutes of cooking time.

Chickpeas
with Mustard Seeds

2 cups dried chickpeas or 2 cans,
about 4 cups when rinsed and drained

1 tablespoon peanut or mustard oil

2 teaspoons ground turmeric

2 teaspoons black mustard seeds

2 onions, chopped

2 garlic cloves, chopped

1 tablespoon dried fenugreek leaves
(optional)

4 tomatoes, peeled,
halved and seeded

3–5 fresh red chiles, halved, seeded if
preferred, then chopped

salt, to taste

fresh methi leaves, to serve (optional)*

SERVES 4

Dried fenugreek leaves (known as "methi" in India and some Asian spice stores) are not as easy to find as the seeds, but they have a unique flavor which scents the dish and makes it something out of the ordinary. If you can't find it in your spice shop, use mint instead, or omit altogether. Use enough chiles to suit your taste.

Put the chickpeas in a bowl, add cold water to cover, and let soak overnight. Next day, drain, put in a flameproof casserole dish, bring to a boil, then transfer to a preheated oven and cook at 300°F for about 2 hours, or until tender (the time will depend on the age of the chickpeas). Add salt, simmer for a further 10 minutes, then drain. If using canned chickpeas, rinse and drain them well.

Heat the oil in the casserole, add the turmeric and mustard seeds, and heat until the seeds pop. Add the onions and garlic and sauté gently until softened and lightly browned. Add the dried fenugreek, if using, tomatoes, and chiles. Cook at a low heat until the tomatoes have melted down to form a sauce.

Return the chickpeas to the casserole, turn to coat with the mixture, cook until hot, then serve, topped with sprigs of fresh methi leaves, if using.

Note Fresh methi leaves are sold in Indian greengrocers. They are cooked and served a little like spinach, but a few sprigs make a delicious garnish. Omit if they are hard to find.

The countries of East and Southeast Asia are as diverse in their cooking styles as Denmark is from Italy or Russia from Spain, so it is remarkable that any similarity exists. But it does: it is especially the cooking methods that unite them, as well as the use of spices, sometimes used sparingly and sometimes vigorously.

Traditionally, ovens are rare and slow casserole cooking is still done on top of a source of heat. In the popular Chinese method of "red cooking" or *hoong sui*, whole pieces of pork or entire fowl are immersed in a pan of highly soy-seasoned liquid and poached gently.

The traditional sandpot is the most recognizable casserole dish in the region. Fairly fragile, it is an earthenware container, glazed inside, and often bound outside with wire to give it strength. Placed directly above hot charcoal, the contents are brought to simmering point and left to cook, often for several hours. A word of warning, however: a naked gas flame, even turned to its lowest, is too violent a source of heat and will crack the pot, so a heat diffuser is essential. Using a sandpot in an ordinary oven is a much safer bet.

Chinese *dumm* steaming is an even slower form of cooking. Meats are first seared in a wok, flavorings added, and the whole turned out into a lidded pot, which is placed on a trivet and lowered into a pan half-filled with hot water which can simmer away all day. This is reminiscent of the French bain-marie way of cooking, showing that a good idea is a good idea anywhere.

Alas, this chapter can only provide a tantalizing taste of the casseroles dishes and cooking methods from this part of the world: I hope they inspire you to search further.

EAST AND SOUTHEAST ASIA

Green Thai Fish Curry

Thai curries are easy to make, quick to cook, and totally delicious. The secret is in the mixture of spices and the freshness of the pastes. You can make the paste in a food processor using ground spices or, if you prefer using whole ones, break them down in a coffee grinder kept solely for that purpose. Store unused paste in the refrigerator.

1¾ cups coconut milk

1½ lb. fish fillets, such as monkfish, cod, or other firm fish

1 tablespoon peanut oil

SPICE PASTE

1 onion, sliced

3 garlic cloves, chopped

6 small hot green chiles, seeded and sliced

2 inches fresh ginger, peeled or scraped and sliced

1 teaspoon ground white pepper

1 teaspoon ground coriander

½ teaspoon ground turmeric

½ teaspoon ground cumin

1 teaspoon shrimp paste (belacan)

1 tablespoon fish sauce

1 stalk of lemongrass, peeled and finely sliced

TO SERVE:

sprigs of Thai basil (optional)

2 limes, halved

fragrant Thai rice or noodles

SERVES 4

Put all the spice paste ingredients in a food processor and work them into a fine purée. Alternatively, use a mortar and pestle. Set aside.

Put the oil in a wok and heat well. Add the spice paste and stir-fry for a few seconds to release the aromas. Add the thick portion from the top of the coconut milk, stir well, and boil to thicken a little.

Add the fish and turn the pieces over in the sauce until they are well coated. Reheat to simmering and cook just until they start to become opaque, about 2 minutes.

Add the remaining coconut milk and continue cooking until the fish is cooked through. Serve topped with Thai basil, if using, plus the halved limes and fragrant Thai rice or noodles.

Note Thai and Vietnamese basil is quite different from ordinary basil. It is sold in Asian food markets—omit it if you can't find it.

Malay Chicken Noodle Soup

2 bundles beanthread or rice noodles such as *ho-fun* or *bahn-pho*, fresh or dried

6 cups Asian chicken stock (page 138) or water

3 lb. whole chicken or 1½ lb. boneless, skinless chicken breasts

8 oz. green beans or Chinese yard-long beans, cut into 3-inch lengths, about 1½ cups

1 carrot, finely sliced

1 zucchini, finely sliced

2 tablespoons peanut oil

salt and freshly ground black pepper

SPICE PASTE

2 stalks of lemongrass

2 tablespoons black pepper, coarsely cracked

2 tablespoons fish sauce, or 1 teaspoon shrimp paste (belacan)

2 teaspoons ground turmeric

8 pink Thai shallots or 2 brown onions, finely chopped

1 inch fresh ginger, peeled and grated

6 garlic cloves, crushed

½ cup blanched almonds

TO SERVE

baby mushrooms, such as enokitaki or hon-shimeji, separated (optional)

4 scallions, finely sliced

4 red chiles, finely sliced

2 lemons, cut in wedges

SERVES 4

You find soups like this in Malaysia, Indonesia, and other parts of Southeast Asia. Use a whole chicken to make the stock, then remove the skin and bone and shred the meat. Alternatively, use ready-made stock and poach chicken breasts separately. Use beanthread or rice vermicelli noodles, not wheat-based ones. Any number of vegetables may be added. You can use a ready-made Thai spice paste, but a blender makes this one in a minute.

If using dried noodles, put them in a bowl and cover with hot water. Let soak for about 30 minutes, then drain and keep in cold water until ready to serve. If using fresh noodles, cut or separate them into strips, soak in hot water for a few minutes, then drain and keep in cold water until ready to serve.

Put the stock or water in a stockpot and bring to a boil. Add the chicken—add more boiling water if the bird is not completely covered by liquid. Poach gently until the chicken is tender, about 1 hour. Remove the chicken to a plate, let cool slightly, discard the skin and bones, then shred the flesh into long pieces. If using chicken breasts, bring the stock to a boil, add the chicken breasts, and poach gently until tender, about 15 minutes. Remove from the stock and shred. Return the stock to a boil, add the beans and carrots, and simmer for 5 minutes or until al dente. Remove with a slotted spoon and plunge them into a bowl of ice water to arrest the cooking. Add the zucchini to the stock and blanch gently until tender, about 1 minute. Remove with a slotted spoon and add to the bowl of ice water. Reserve the stock. When all the vegetables are cold, remove them from the ice water and reserve.

To make the spice paste, cut the top off the lemongrass, keeping the white part only. Peel off the 2 outer leaves, and finely slice the rest. Put in a small blender or food processor with the other spice paste ingredients and grind to a coarse paste. Alternatively, use a mortar and pestle. Set aside.

Heat the oil in a wok or skillet, add the spice paste, and sauté gently until fragrant. Add the reserved stock, shredded chicken, blanched beans, carrots, and zucchini and heat until very hot. Taste and adjust the seasoning. Drain the noodles and divide between 4 large bowls. Ladle the chicken and stock over the noodles and serve, topped with the scallions, chiles, and mushrooms, if using. Serve with lemon wedges for squeezing.

A recipe from the border of China and the former Indo-China—the tang of orange mixed with crushed yellow bean sauce is a gorgeous combination and the whole dish can be prepared in advance up to the point where it is put into the oven. A word of warning—the sauce around the duck, before it goes in the oven, must be very thick, because the bok choy or cabbage gives off so much water that the dish can easily become diluted.

Braised Duck and Ginger

4 large duck breasts, cut into thick slices

5 teaspoons cornstarch

½ cup yellow bean paste or sauce

2 tablespoons Shao Xing (sweet Chinese rice wine) or mirin

2 teaspoons sugar

freshly ground black pepper

1 onion, finely chopped

2 tablespoons peanut oil

4 inches fresh ginger, peeled and thickly sliced

2 garlic cloves, crushed

zest of 1 orange or 1 tangerine

2 tablespoons dark soy sauce

4 baby bok choy, halved lengthwise, or ½ Chinese cabbage, sliced crosswise

4 scallions, sliced, to serve

SERVES 4

Put the duck in a bowl, sprinkle with 1 teaspoon of the cornstarch, and mix until coated.

Heat a wok or skillet, add the duck (without adding any oil), and stir-fry to release the fat and firm up the meat. Remove with a slotted spoon and return the duck to the bowl.

Put the bean paste or sauce in a small bowl, add ½ cup water, the rice wine or mirin, sugar, and freshly ground black pepper, and mix well.

Add the onion to the wok or pan, then add the bean paste mixture. Simmer for about 30 seconds, then pour the mixture over the duck. Reheat the wok with the oil and sauté the ginger and garlic to release their flavor. Return the duck and its sauce to the wok, add the zest, and simmer lightly until most of the water has evaporated.

Mix the remaining cornstarch with 2 tablespoons water and the soy sauce, stir into the wok, and bring to a boil, stirring.

Line a Chinese sandpot with the bok choy or Chinese cabbage, arrange the duck over the top, then pour over the sauce. Cook a preheated oven at 350°F for 10 minutes until tender. Remove from the oven and, if the leaves have given off too much liquid, pour it into a saucepan or wok and boil until it thickens again to a coating consistency. Return to the pot, sprinkle with the scallions, and serve with other Chinese dishes.

"Red-cooking" is a braising method used for whole ducks or chickens, or large pieces of pork—and the red color comes from soy sauce. This dish uses a great deal of soy, but it can be used again and again (freeze between uses). Use dark soy, which is less salty than light.

Red-Cooked Pork

2 lb. pork spareribs
or loin, or shoulder roast

RED STOCK

2 cups Chinese rice wine

3 cups chicken stock
(page 134 or 138) or water

2 cups dark soy sauce

2 tablespoons rice vinegar

2 cinnamon sticks

1 inch fresh ginger, sliced

zest of 1 tangerine or orange

2 whole star anise

6 scallions

SERVES 6–8

Put all the stock ingredients into a large flameproof casserole and bring to a boil. Add the pork, return to a boil, then simmer on top of the stove or in a preheated oven at 350°F for 45 minutes if using pork loin, or 1½ hours if using pork shoulder or spareribs. When the meat is very tender, carefully lift it out onto on a wooden board and, using a Chinese cleaver, cut it into thick slices or bite-sized chunks. Serve with other Chinese dishes such as noodles, stir-fried vegetables, or steamed rice.

Notes Some of the stock is served with the dish, the rest is kept and used over and over again, improving in flavor each time a new dish is cooked in it: if you don't plan to make this often, the stock may be frozen.

Although red-cooked pork is a typical Chinese dish—and perfect served with other Chinese dishes—it is also delicious served with mashed potatoes or mashed white beans, with a little of the stock drizzled over.

Variation For extra flavor, marinate the pork overnight in the refrigerator in a Southeast Asian spice paste. Using a blender or mortar and pestle, grind 1 teaspoon ground coriander, 1 teaspoon crushed white peppercorns, 4 crushed garlic cloves, 2 stalks of lemongrass, peeled and chopped, 2 inches fresh ginger, peeled and chopped, 4 red chiles, seeded and chopped, 2 teaspoon shrimp paste (optional), 1 tablespoon sunflower oil, and 2 teaspoons rice vinegar. Spread the mixture over the pork and marinate overnight in the refrigerator.

Eggplant Sandpot

1 small eggplant or
4 Chinese eggplants

½ medium bunch broccoli

1½ teaspoons salt

1½ teaspoons sugar

1 carrot, cut in matchsticks, or 8 baby
carrots, halved lengthwise

3 tablespoons peanut oil

1 tablespoon sesame oil

1 inch fresh ginger, peeled and sliced

2 garlic cloves, crushed

8 oz. canned water chestnuts,
rinsed and drained

1 tablespoon yellow bean paste,
thinned with ⅛ cup water

1 tablespoon dark soy sauce

1 tablespoon rice vinegar

½ cup vegetable stock (page 133)

2 teaspoons cornstarch,
mixed with 1 tablespoon water

2 scallions, finely sliced

SERVES 4

If using a whole eggplant, trim and cut it into finger-sized strips. If using Chinese eggplants, halve them lengthwise. Snap the florets off the broccoli, peel the stalk, and cut it into finger-sized strips.

Bring a large saucepan of water to a boil, then add ½ teaspoon of the salt and ½ teaspoon of the sugar. Add the broccoli florets and boil for 2 minutes. Remove the florets with a slotted spoon and put into a bowl of cold water.

Add the broccoli stems and carrots to the boiling water and blanch for 5 minutes. Remove with a slotted spoon and add to the bowl of cold water. Drain the vegetables through a colander, reserving the cooking water.

Put the peanut oil and 1 teaspoon of the sesame oil in a wok or skillet, add the ginger and garlic, and stir-fry for 2 minutes. Add the drained vegetables and water chestnuts and stir-fry for 2 minutes to coat with the oil and make them glisten. Transfer to a sandpot or other casserole dish.

Add the remaining sesame oil to the wok, then add the diluted yellow bean paste, soy sauce, vinegar, stock, the remaining sugar and salt, and ½ cup of the blanching water. Bring to a boil. Mix the cornstarch with 1 tablespoon water, then stir into the wok.

Pour over the vegetables and sprinkle with sliced scallions. Cover and transfer to a preheated oven at 350°F and cook for 20 minutes or until the liquid bubbles through. Serve with other Chinese dishes.

Asian eggplants come in all shapes, sizes, and colors. They range from tiny, green, grape-like bunches to the egg-shaped white ones which gave them their name—and from the familiar large, purple ones to the Chinese varieties, about 3 inches long, which are ideal for this recipe.

Monks' Vegetables

Vegetarian diets were never hugely popular in China. The monasteries were the main proponents of the vegetarian lifestyle—and there aren't many monks left in the People's Republic. However, I love this recipe and I'm certainly not a vegetarian. It is so good that any meat would utterly ruin its flavor—and yet it has the satisfying effect of a meat dish. Stir-fry the ingredients in the order given, so that you build up the pot in the recommended order. If you haven't got one ingredient, choose something similar so their textures give a good balance of crunch and softness. Make sure to give the tofu a very light dusting of cornstarch so the pieces will brown deliciously all over without sticking.

Monks' Vegetables
step-by-step

½ Chinese cabbage, leaves separated

1 cup peanut oil

4 carrots, peeled and finely sliced diagonally

8 oz. canned sliced bamboo shoots, drained

1 cup fresh shiitake mushrooms, halved

8 oz. canned sliced water chestnuts, drained

4 baby bok choy, halved lengthwise

2 blocks firm tofu, cut into 1-inch cubes

3 tablespoons cornstarch, for dusting

SAUCE

2 tablespoons crushed yellow bean sauce diluted with ⅓ cup water

2 tablespoons light soy sauce

2 tablespoons dark soy sauce

2 tablespoons hoisin sauce

2 tablespoons sugar

1 cup water or vegetable stock

½ cup Shao Xing (Chinese sweetened rice wine) or medium sherry

SERVES 4

1 Bring a large saucepan of water to a boil, add the Chinese cabbage leaves, and blanch for 1 minute. Remove, plunge into a large bowl of ice water, then drain.

2 Cut out and discard the white stalks. Put the leaves one on top of the other on a dry cloth (arrange them with stalk ends on alternate sides).

6 Dust the tofu with the flour, in several batches (do this just before cooking).

7 Heat ½ cup of the oil in the wok or skillet (it must be very hot or the tofu will stick). Sauté the tofu pieces in the oil until well browned. Remove with a slotted spoon, then drain.

3 Roll up the leaves like a sushi into a cylinder and press hard to squeeze out the water.

4 Remove from the cloth and cut the rolls into 2-inch lengths. Set aside.

Note This cabbage preparation is based on a Japanese original, but is a terrific way to include lots of leaves in the dish without taking up huge amounts of room.

5 Heal 1 tablespoon of the oil in a wok or skillet until it begins to smoke. Stir-fry all the vegetables, except the cabbage and bok choy, one at a time in the order shown, removing each one to a plate before adding the next. Add more oil as required and reheat it each time before cooking the next batch.

8 Put a layer of fried tofu in a Chinese sandpot or ceramic casserole dish. Add the carrots, bamboo shoots, mushrooms, water chestnuts, bok choy, and cabbage rolls.

9 Mix the sauce ingredients in a measuring cup or bowl and pour over the vegetables. Cover with a lid and set aside to marinate for about 30 minutes or until you are ready to cook the final dish.

10 Put the sandpot or casserole into a cold oven, turn the heat to 400°F for 20 minutes, or until boiling, then reduce the heat to 275°F and simmer for about 3 minutes for the sauce to bubble through. Serve with rice or noodles.

Australians and New Zealanders can trace their ancestors to almost every part of the world, so their casserole dishes reflect that multi-ethnic past, a veritable Cook's Tour of the globe. You find lamb ragouts from Greece, seafood soups from the Mediterranean and Southeast Asia, and beef braises from Britain.

The first settlers were English, Scots, and Irish, so dishes from Britain form the basis of Antipodean cuisine. The face of Australian food was changed forever after World War II, when "New Australians" came from Greece, Italy, Lebanon, the Baltic States, Central and Eastern Europe, and Jewish people from all over. The result was a plethora of new and vibrant ingredients and interesting cooking. Further change occurred with the post-1972 influx from the Middle East, Vietnam, Indonesia, and other parts of Southeast Asia. To the traditional stews and braises of Europe were added dishes like curry from Thailand, *pho* from Vietnam, and *laksa* from Malaysia.

Australian cooks make use of incredible ingredients: beef and lamb that give new meaning to the words "free range;" unusual local game such as kangaroo and buffalo; fish and seafood of extraordinary variety, freshness, and quality; and fruits, vegetables, and spices produced by farmers working in a huge range of climates. Added to that are the legendary wines of Australia and New Zealand—good to drink and very good for cooking.

This is an area where local cuisine is being constantly reborn, in a climate of absolute passion about food. All in all, this must be one of the most exciting places in the world to cook and eat today.

AUSTRALIA AND NEW ZEALAND

Australian Seafood Stew

All countries with a coastline develop their own traditional forms of fish stew and Australia is no exception. A marvelous variety of fish and seafood, plus a vibrant multi-ethnic tradition, make for a unique and fascinating version of this universal dish. There is a strong influence from Southeast Asia, but the style is reminiscent of France's generous Bordeaux *fruits de mer* dishes. Monkfish is not caught in Australian waters, but its texture is very suited to fish stews: substitute any similar local fish with firm white flesh. Choose any combination of shellfish such as clams or mussels, plus crustacea such as shrimp or lobsters. Just remember, don't cook any kind of seafood for very long, or it will be come tough and lose its flavor, while fish will disintegrate. Cook gently and only until the flesh becomes opaque.

Australian Seafood Stew

step-by-step

2 tablespoons peanut, canola, or safflower oil

2 large onions, finely sliced

2 inches fresh ginger, finely chopped

3 large garlic cloves, crushed

2 stalks of lemongrass, very finely sliced

6 kaffir lime leaves or juice of 1 lime

1 cup white wine

about 2 lb. mussels, well scrubbed, with beards removed

20 clams

4 cups fish stock

2 fresh red chiles, halved lengthwise

4 small crayfish or lobster tails (optional)

1 lb. monkfish or other firm fish, skinned and cut into 1-inch chunks

8 large shrimp

salt, to taste

TO SERVE

4 scallions, sliced

2 red chiles, sliced

1 cup cilantro, torn

SERVES 4

1 Heat the oil in a wok or casserole, add the onion, ginger, garlic, lemongrass, and kaffir lime leaves or lime juice, and sauté until the onions are softened and translucent. Add the wine and 1 cup water and bring to a boil.

2 Add the mussels* and clams, put on the lid, and steam until they open, shaking the pan from time to time.

*Make sure all the mussels have been scraped, rinsed, and the beards pulled away and discarded before cooking. Tap the mussels against the kitchen counter and discard any that don't close. Clams should also close when tapped.

3 Remove the opened shellfish with a slotted spoon, put in a bowl, and keep them warm. If they were very sandy, you may need to strain the cooking liquid, then return it to the pan. Add the stock and bring to a boil.

4 Add the chiles and crayfish or lobster tails, if using, and simmer until the shells change color and the flesh is opaque all the way through (the time will depend on the size of the tails). When cooked, remove from the pan and cut in half lengthwise. Add to the mussels and keep them warm.

5 Add the fish and shrimp and poach gently until they are opaque all the way through—do not overcook or the shrimp will be tough. Taste the liquid and adjust the seasoning. (Take care, because mussels are often salty and it's easy to add too much.)

6 Divide the seafood between 4 big soup bowls, bring the liquid to a boil, then ladle into the bowls.

7 Top with the scallions, chiles, and torn cilantro. Serve the stew with Chinese soup spoons and chopsticks, and a small dish of sliced chiles for people to help themselves.

Meat cooked on the bone has a very different texture from the boned type where the meat can shrink back unimpeded into a tight ball. The meat remains stretched as it cooks and has a tender, far more open texture.

Braised Lamb Shanks
with Orange and Marmalade

4 lamb shanks

¼ cup olive oil

3 garlic cloves, sliced

freshly squeezed juice
of 2 oranges, about 1 cup

½ cup dry white wine

zest of 1 lemon, removed
with a zester or potato peeler

3 tablespoons
bitter orange marmalade

½ cup chicken stock (page 134)
or water

salt and freshly ground black pepper

SERVES 4

Preheat the broiler until very hot. Brush the shanks with 3 tablespoons of the oil and season well, then broil, turning them as necessary until well-browned all over.

Heat the remaining oil in a flameproof casserole, add the garlic, and brown gently without burning. Add the shanks, orange juice, white wine, and lemon zest. Bring to a boil on top of the stove, cover with a lid, then transfer to a preheated oven and cook at 350°F for 1 hour, or until the meat pulls away from the bones.

Using a slotted spoon, transfer the shanks to a plate or bowl and keep them warm. Transfer the casserole to the top of the stove over a medium heat.

Add the marmalade to the casserole, stir until well blended, bring to a boil, and simmer until the liquid has been reduced to a coating glaze.

Return the shanks to the casserole and turn in the glaze until well coated. Serve on heated dinner plates. Add the stock to the casserole, stir to scrape up the flavored bits left in the pan, then spoon over the shanks and serve.

Oxtail makes a rich stew and is popular everywhere, especially in Australia, with its huge beef industry. Oxtail's natural gelatin gives this dish a delicious, sticky, glutinous texture. However, it also has an excessive amount of fat on the biggest sections, most of which must be cut away before cooking and lifted off when the cooking is complete. You can also chill the casserole overnight and remove the fat when cold.

Oxtail in Red Wine

½ cup olive oil

3 tablespoons all-purpose flour

2 large onions, sliced

4 lb. oxtail, trimmed of fat

2 carrots, cut into chunks

4 tomatoes, chopped

2–3 sprigs of thyme

1 celery stalk, sliced

3 bay leaves

10 peppercorns

⅔ cup brandy

1 bottle red wine, 750 ml

7 cups beef stock (page 136)

salt and freshly ground black pepper

TO SERVE

freshly cooked vegetables, such as baby carrots, turnips, and parsnips and green vegetables such as broccoli

mashed potatoes

SERVES 4–6

To make a roux, put 3 tablespoons of the oil in a small skillet, add the flour, and cook gently, stirring, until it becomes a nutty brown color.

Heat another 3 tablespoons of the oil in a large, flameproof casserole, add the onion, and sauté until golden. Add the smaller pieces of oxtail, carrots, tomatoes, thyme, celery, bay leaves, and peppercorns. Sauté until browned. Transfer to a bowl and keep them warm.

Rinse the casserole, return to the heat, and add the remaining oil. Add the larger pieces of oxtail and sauté until browned on all sides. Pour off the fat.

Warm the brandy in a small saucepan, light with a match, and pour over the meat. Shake the casserole gently, keeping the flame alight as long as possible to burn off all the alcohol.

Transfer the meat to the bowl of vegetables and add the wine to the casserole. Bring to a boil and cook until it becomes syrupy and almost disappears. Stir in the roux, then the stock. Bring to a boil, stirring all the time to make a sauce. Add salt and pepper, then gently mix in all the meat and vegetables. Transfer to a preheated oven and cook at 300°F for at least 3 hours, or until the meat is falling off the bone.

Remove from the oven and set aside for about 10 minutes to let the fat rise to the surface. Spoon off as much fat as you can. Alternatively, let cool, then chill overnight.

About 1 hour before serving, remove any fat from the surface and reheat the stew, adding a little boiling water if the sauce has become too dry. Taste and adjust the seasoning. Transfer the large pieces of meat to a bowl and strain the gravy over. Discard the vegetables and any small bones.

Gently return the stew to the casserole and top with your choice of freshly cooked vegetables. Serve with lots of mashed potatoes for mopping up the sauce.

It may seem odd to find Vietnamese food as an example of casserole cooking in Australia, especially with French bread, but Vietnamese immigrants have had an exciting effect on food Down Under. In addition, their baking prowess is a legacy of the French colonial period and they have opened some of Australia's best bread bakeries. This beef casserole is eaten as street food or at home—served with crusty baguettes or rice.

Vietnamese Beef with Baguettes

1 stalk of lemongrass, peeled and finely chopped

leaves from 3 sprigs of mint, chopped

2 tablespoons fish sauce

1 teaspoon brown sugar

1 inch fresh ginger, peeled and grated

1 red chile, seeded and chopped

2 garlic cloves, crushed

freshly ground black pepper

2 lb. boneless beef (foreshank or chuck), cut into 1-inch cubes

about 2 tablespoons peanut oil

2 tablespoons tomato purée

3 tomatoes, peeled, seeded, and chopped, about 1 lb.

4 cups water or Vietnamese Beef Stock (page 139)

TO SERVE

6 scallions, shredded

sprigs of mint

crusty baguettes

SERVES 4–6

Put the lemongrass, mint, fish sauce, sugar, ginger, chile, garlic, and lots of freshly ground black pepper in a bowl and mix well.

Add the beef and turn to coat. Cover and marinate in the refrigerator for about 2 hours or overnight.

Heat the oil in a casserole dish, then add the beef in batches and sauté until browned on all sides. Using a slotted spoon, remove each batch to a plate and keep it warm while you cook the remainder.

Return all the beef to the pan, add the tomato purée and tomatoes, and cook for 3–4 minutes until they start to break down. Add 4 cups water or beef stock and bring to a boil. Reduce the heat and simmer for about 2 hours until the meat is spoon-tender and the sauce rich but not too thick.

Serve in small bowls, topped with shredded scallions and mint sprigs, accompanied by crusty baguettes for mopping up the juices.

The original of this chicken dish came from a gourmet food writer in Melbourne twenty-five years ago and then, the cook-in sauce seemed then to be well ahead of its time. Nowadays, it is more normal to mix Western ingredients (Italian olives, pimento, and basil) and Eastern (soy sauce, lemon, and honey) to make a fusion whole. Sometimes fusions don't work, but this one does, and it's typical of the culinary cross-pollination that happens in Australia and New Zealand. The sweet potato base mops up all the cooking juices from the chicken.

Chicken and Sweet Potatoes
with Honey, Soy, and Lemon

⅓ cup olive oil

2 sweet potatoes, about 1 lb. cut into ½-inch rounds

4 chicken legs (thighs and drumsticks)

1 cup pimento-stuffed green olives

½ cup dry white wine

¼ cup honey

2 cups basil leaves

6 garlic cloves, crushed

¼ cup soy sauce

finely grated zest and juice of 2 lemons

SERVES 4

Heat ¼ cup of the oil in a large skillet, add the sweet potatoes and sauté until lightly browned. Transfer to an ovenproof casserole.

Add the remaining oil to the skillet, add the chicken legs, and sauté until browned all over. Put them on top of the sweet potatoes in the casserole.

Put the olives, wine, honey, basil, garlic, soy sauce, lemon zest, and juice into a food processor or blender and purée until smooth. Pour the mixture over the chicken.

Transfer to a preheated oven and cook at 400°F for about 30 minutes, or until the casserole comes to a boil, then reduce the heat to 300°F and simmer for 30 minutes, or until the chicken is tender.

Bell Pepper Chile Tian

with Goat Cheese and Chorizo

This Australian and New Zealand version of a Provençal tian is cooked in a wide, shallow, open casserole dish. Peppers are called "capsicums" in Australia, which is the correct name for this whole group of vegetables.

4 red bell peppers

2 yellow or orange bell peppers

2 red onions, finely chopped

½ cup extra virgin olive oil, plus extra for brushing and drizzling

2 small mild chorizo sausages, finely sliced

a handful of basil leaves

16 cherry tomatoes, halved

1–2 medium-hot fresh red chiles, seeded and finely sliced (optional)

about 8 oz. mature goat cheese, cut into 12 chunks

salt, preferably sea salt flakes, and freshly ground black pepper

PESTO

1 large bunch of fresh basil

a large handful of parsley leaves

¼ cup olive oil

¼ cup pine nuts

2 garlic cloves, crushed

1 cup grated Parmesan cheese

TO SERVE

salad leaves

sprigs of basil

lemon wedges

char-grilled Italian bread

SERVES 4

To make the pesto, put the basil, parsley, olive oil, pine nuts, and garlic in a blender and process until smooth. Add the Parmesan, then blend again.

Cut the bell peppers in half lengthwise through the stalk. Carefully remove the cores.

Put the peppers in a plastic bag, add the ½ cup olive oil, salt, and pepper, then shake until well coated with oil.

Brush a shallow tian or casserole dish with extra olive oil and add the peppers, cut side up, cramming them close together. Put a slice of chorizo, a basil leaf, a halved cherry tomato, a spoonful of pesto, some onion, a little chile, if using, and a chunk of goat cheese in each pepper half. Drizzle more olive oil over the top.

Cook in a preheated oven at 400°F for about 30 minutes, or until all the peppers are tender and crispy brown at the edges and the cheese is melted and bubbling.

Serve on small plates with a tangle of salad leaves, extra fresh basil leaves scattered over the top, and wedges of lemon for squeezing. Char-grilled Italian bread is perfect for mopping up the delicious juices.

Basic Preparations

Some useful basic principles of casserole cooking found in many cuisines include:

Browning onions

Onions contain natural sugars. When heated to a high temperature, those sugars start to turn brown and develop delicious caramel flavor and color, just like loose sugar. This will add considerably to the quality of flavor and appearance of stocks and casseroles. Over-browning produces a bitter taste.

Browning meats

Always brown meat in batches. Why? Because when meat is sautéed, the fibers shrink and squeeze out the meat juices. These in turn form a concentrated meat "glace" or glaze. However, if the source of heat is not strong enough to reduce the liquid as it appears, it collects in the pan, boiling and toughening the meat. The answer is to brown the meat in smaller batches and use the largest pan practicable so boiling doesn't occur.

Thickening

Wheat flour

Flour is used in sauces and gravies to thicken the liquid. Mixed in equal quantities with butter, oil, or fat, it is called "manié." When this mixture is cooked, it is called a roux and loses its raw, floury taste. With longer cooking, the roux turns brown—as in many Cajun recipes—and loses some of its thickening properties. This last browning must be done very slowly so that the flour colors evenly, otherwise it will "catch" and burn in places.

Cornstarch, rice flour, and potato flour

These starches do not contain the gluten of wheat. In casserole cooking, they have several advantages:

• Their thickening process leaves a clearer sauce.
• They absorb fats floating on the surface of liquids.
• They thicken to a maximum just below boiling point, but should preferably be boiled to achieve the best flavor.

Cooking with wines and spirits, alcohols, and vinegars

These are among the best flavoring agents found in the pantry. They are acidulators with preservative qualities.

The correct way to use them is to boil off their unwanted esters and concentrate their flavors. This is usually done when a recipe requires a pan to be "deglazed" in wine, spirits, or vinegar. The result is that any cooked particles or meat juices are dissolved into the deglazing liquid and flavors retained.

Beer often needs sugar added to counteract its bitterness.

Cooking with spices

Spices are used as flavorings and preservatives and, preferably, should be ground (like coffee beans) just before use. Roasting them in a dry skillet or in fat or oil releases their aromas and matures their flavor. A mixture of spices is known in India as a "masala" and great care is taken to create special combinations suited to each dish.

In many Southeast Asian cuisines, the spices are usually ground into pastes using a mortar and pestle (a modern coffee grinder kept for the purpose is a good lazy-cook's substitute). The spice pastes are then sautéed in oil or in a small amount of coconut cream to release their aromas before the rest of the ingredients are added.

Saffron, whether powder or threads, is usually lightly toasted, then ground or steeped in water to draw out its flavor and color. This will take several hours and should be done before being added to the dish.

Vegetable Stock

Vegetable stock should be made with a range of vegetables to produce a clear, clean liquid, full of flavor. The choice of ingredients is crucial—avoid starchy vegetables like potatoes and parsnips, which will cloud the stock, and those with flavor too dominating, such as the cabbage family. Wine is acid and counteracts the sweetness of cooked onions: it also clears the stock. I sometimes add a garlic clove and a twist of tangerine or orange zest with a small bunch of lemon thyme for the last ten minutes, to lift the flavor out of the ordinary, but these are optional. Don't add salt to stock—add it to the dish as required.

2 tomatoes

1 leek, white part only

1 carrot

1 onion

2 shallots

a bouquet garni (a bundle of herbs, tied up with kitchen twine)

10 peppercorns

½ cup white wine

MAKES 3 CUPS

Wash the vegetables (peeling is optional). Chop them coarsely and put everything into a large non-reactive (stainless steel or enamel) Dutch oven. Cover with about 5 cups water and add the wine. Simmer for 2 hours and then bring to a rolling boil for a few moments. Pour through a fine strainer or cheesecloth. Chill and freeze.

Alternatively, for a different flavor, heat a little oil in the pan first, then sauté the vegetables until their sugar caramelizes and they brown. Do not let the onions become too dark, or their sugar will burn and give a bitter taste. This stock tends to be a bit cloudy.

Microwave Stock

I have made a similar stock in the microwave, using less water and at a LOW power: it took about half the time.

Chicken Stock

It is always a good thing to have chicken stock available as it has so many applications, ranging from aspics to soups and casseroles, and will never be wasted. This method will produce an excellent white stock, as neither the vegetables nor the meats and bones have been browned. The optional wine or vinegar helps coagulate the loose proteins, making them easier to strain out.

Clarifying stocks

Really sparklingly clear stocks are usually reserved for making consommés or aspics, as a little sediment does no harm to sauces thickened with flours or other liaisons. However, with some Asian dishes, a beautifully clear stock is called for and then the care must start right from the beginning as a fatty, opaque stock cannot be rectified—or almost never. Follow steps 1–4 here, then pass the liquid through a fine strainer or cheesecloth. Put 6 oz. totally lean, finely hand-chopped meat, chicken, or fish (according to the stock being cleared) in a bowl, then add 3 lightly beaten egg whites for every 8–10 cups stock. Heat the stock just to boiling point, stir in the egg white mixture, and simmer for 30 minutes without disturbing it other than by opening a small blowhole to release steam buildup. During this time, any floating impurities rise to the surface and stick to the albumen in the egg white, which cooks into a solid mat. Carefully remove the mat, then pour the clear liquid through a cheesecloth-lined strainer into a bowl.

2 carcasses uncooked chicken, 2 lb. wings, or 1 turkey drumstick, sliced

any giblets or trimmings such as wingtips from the chickens

4 carrots, sliced

1 leek, well cleaned and sliced

1 onion, sliced or chopped

1 celery stalk

1 teaspoon black peppercorns

1 bay leaf

1 sprig of thyme

2–3 parsley stalks

2 tablespoons white wine or 1 tablespoon white wine vinegar

5 tablespoons unsalted butter (optional)

MAKES 6 CUPS

1 Chop the chicken carcasses into several large pieces, put in a Dutch oven with any giblets or trimmings, cover with cold water, and skim off any fat that rises to the surface. Bring to a gentle simmer without boiling and skim off any foam that rises to the surface.

2 Add all the prepared vegetables, herbs, peppercorns, and white wine or white wine vinegar, return to simmering, and cook for 1½ hours.

Alternatively, heat the butter, if using, in a skillet, add the vegetables, and cook until lightly browned. Add to the chicken in the Dutch oven and proceed as before.

White Stock

A classic white stock contains a variety of meat and bones. Veal and veal bones are preferred ingredients. Should a boiling fowl be available, it gives a most flavorful stock, but it needs to be de-fatted thoroughly (see the method for Asian Chicken Stock, page 138). If unavailable, use plenty of raw chicken wings or wingtips and carcasses, if available, or a turkey drumstick. A pig's foot will produce the necessary gelatin in the absence of veal bones, but enough chicken bones will also do the trick. Some trimmings from pork or lamb are acceptable, but not in any great proportion to the rest of the bones because the stock produced from these tastes a little sweet. Beef trimmings are excellent. The method is the same as for chicken stock.

3 Pour the stock through a strainer.

Note For a clearer stock, strain through cheesecloth (although this will take longer).

4 Cool the stock quickly, then freeze. After 3–4 hours, the solidified fat can be scraped off with a spoon. Return the stock to the pan, bring to a boil, and simmer until reduced to the required intensity of flavor. Freeze in conveniently sized containers.

Slow-Cooker Stock

A slow cooker is a convenient way to make stock. Put the raw chicken carcasses in a slow cooker without any vegetables, cover with cold water and a lid, switch onto the higher setting, and cook for at least 8 hours or overnight. Strain, cool, and freeze. Scrape off all the fat and bring to a boil to reduce, if necessary, to about 4 cups.

Beef Stock

When the sugars in the meats, bones, or vegetables are caramelized through roasting or sautéing, the result is what is known as a "brown stock." It has a richer color and a little more flavor. As with all stock making, there are a few basic rules:

• Never continue boiling a stock once it has reached a boil. Just keep it hot enough for the steam to find a blowhole in the fat and puff gently through. The reason is that, as the fat dissolves and floats to the surface, it makes a transparent layer on the top. If this is broken up continually by lots of bubbles breaking the surface, the fat is drawn back down into the body of the stock, where it gradually combines and emulsifies with the liquid, producing an opaque and fatty stock. A little boiling at the beginning doesn't hurt, but a vigorous one halfway through is not good at all.

• Use rib bones, not marrow bones as are usually recommended—marrow bones will make the stock fatty.

• Never add salt to a stock—keep the salt for the final dish.

10 lb. mixed beef bones (see left)

2 lb. shank crosscuts of beef and beef trimmings (optional)

2 lb. onions, coarsely chopped

2 lb. carrots, cut into chunks

1 large leek, split, well washed and drained, then thickly sliced

2 tomatoes, halved

a bouquet garni (a bundle of herbs tied up with kitchen twine)

⅔ cup red wine or wine vinegar

MAKES 4–6 CUPS

1 Put the bones in 2 roasting pans and roast in a preheated oven at 400°F for 25 minutes—they should brown slowly.

2 Add the vegetables and increase the oven heat as high as it will go, about 500°F, to caramelize the juices left in the pan and brown the vegetables, about 5 minutes. Do not let the bones char or blacken.

3 When the bones and vegetables are nicely browned, transfer to a Dutch oven, add the bouquet garni, cover with cold water, and bring to a boil.

4 Pour off any fat left in the roasting pans, add the wine or vinegar, and boil until reduced by two-thirds. Mix in 1 cup water and pour into the Dutch oven. The acid helps coagulate the albumin that forms as foam on top of the liquid and should be skimmed off. Simmer, uncovered, for about 4 hours, making sure the liquid does not boil.

5 Strain the stock into a bowl. Discard the bones and vegetables. If you pour it through cheesecloth, the stock will be clearer, but it will take longer. If the pan has a tap, drain off most of the stock, being careful to leave behind the fat which is lying on the surface. To cool the stock quickly, put the bowl into a tub of ice water.

6 Chill the stock for about 4 hours or overnight. It will form a lid of fat which can be lifted off and discarded. Return the stock to the pan, bring to a boil, and reduce to strengthen the flavor. Cool, divide into small containers (about 1 cup), and store in the refrigerator or freeze. To make a glace, reduce still further until syrupy.

Asian Stocks

Casserole recipes in some parts of the world, such as the Middle East and India, are usually made with water instead of stock as their poaching liquid. In East and Southeast Asia, however, a wide range of stocks is used to add flavor, or even as the main ingredient in curries and soups, especially light soups with quick-cooking seafood, vegetables, or noodles. Flavor and clarity are prized—in the first recipe, you will find an excellent technique for clarifying stock.

Chicken Stock

A delicious light chicken stock of very good quality—fat-free and very clear.

2 lb. chicken carcasses, wings, or wingtips
2 inches fresh ginger, sliced
8 oz. shallots or large-bulbed scallions
8 garlic cloves, lightly crushed
10 peppercorns
6 cilantro stalks with leaves

MAKES ABOUT 6 CUPS

Remove and discard all fat from the carcasses. Chop coarsely. Put into a large, stainless steel or enamel saucepan. Add 3 quarts cold water. Heat to simmering, but do not let boil. Skim any foam off the surface. Add all the other ingredients and heat to simmering, letting the surface break with slow bubbles in several places to release the steam.

Simmer for about 2½ hours. Drain off the liquid—which should still be clear—through a cheesecloth-lined strainer into a bowl. Cool, then freeze until the fat has congealed on the surface.

Scrape off the fat and discard. While the liquid is frozen, tilt the bowl and pour a little boiling water over the surface to wash off any fat still clinging to it or to the sides of the bowl. Transfer the stock into a clean saucepan, bring to a rolling boil, and reduce to 6 cups, or until the strength is to your liking. Use immediately or freeze in convenient quantities.

Thai-Style Stock

This simple stock can be made with all chicken or chicken and pork. Use it as a basis for soups and curries.

about 3 lb. chicken carcasses, chopped into 4–6 pieces, or wings

about 1 lb. lean pork with bones, cut into large chunks

a handful of cilantro, with stalks and roots if possible

a large pinch of salt

MAKES ABOUT 4 CUPS

Put the chicken, pork, and cilantro in a large saucepan, then add the salt and about 2 quarts water. Bring to a boil and skim off any foam that rises to the surface. Repeat the skimming several times, then reduce the heat to a gentle simmer and cook for about 1 hour.

Remove from the heat and let cool. When cool, pour gently through a fine strainer, so as not to disturb too much of the sediment. Discard the bones and sediment.

Chill, preferably overnight, then scrape off the fat from the top of the stock.

Use immediately or freeze in convenient quantities.

Southeast Asian Chicken or Pork Stock

A basic stock made from any available poultry or meat. The sugar-salt-spice combination is very common in Vietnam. When the stock is strained, reserve any small pieces of meat or chicken and use them in sandwiches or salads.

4 lb. chicken carcasses or pork bones, or a combination of both

1 inch fresh ginger, peeled and sliced

1 shallot or onion, cut into wedges

a large pinch of salt

a pinch of sugar

MAKES ABOUT 6 CUPS

Put the bones in a large saucepan and cover with cold water.

Bring slowly to a boil, then boil for 10–15 minutes, skimming off the foam several times.

Reduce the heat, add the ginger, shallot or onion, salt, and sugar, then simmer for about 2 hours.

Carefully pour through a fine strainer, discarding the bones, flavorings, and sediment. Pick off and reserve any shreds of meat. Chill and remove the fat. Use immediately or freeze in convenient quantities.

Vietnamese Beef Stock

The basis of the legendary Vietnamese beef noodle soup, *pho bo*, and of many other soups, this is a useful stock.

2 lb. shin of beef, with bones, cut into 1-inch slices

1 lb. beef shank crosscuts

1 inch fresh ginger, peeled and sliced

a pinch of salt

3 tablespoons fish sauce

2 whole star anise

1 cinnamon stick, broken

2 onions, sliced

MAKES ABOUT 4 CUPS

Put the bones in a large saucepan, cover completely with cold water, and bring to a boil. Boil for 15 minutes, skimming off the foam every few minutes. When the foam stops rising, reduce the heat, add the crosscuts of beef, and simmer for about 2 hours.

Add the ginger, salt, fish sauce, star anise, cinnamon stick, and onions and continue simmering for 30 minutes.

Carefully pour through a fine strainer, discarding the bones, flavorings, and sediment. Reserve the meat for another dish. Chill, remove the fat, and use the stock within 3 days or freeze in convenient quantities.

Fish Stock

The best fish bones are those from flat fish such as turbot, sole, and halibut. Non-oily round fish bones from cod or monkfish may be used, but do not use oily fish such as mackerel, trout, salmon, sardines, pilchards, or any smoked fish. If you wish to use salmon bones for a salmon-flavored stock, before using it you must skim off any globules of orange-colored oil floating on the surface. Always use fish stocks as soon as possible because the flavor will deteriorate under refrigeration.

10 lb. lean, white-fleshed fish bones
6 tablespoons butter
2 onions, chopped
3 celery stalks, chopped
10 parsley stalks
10 peppercorns
1 bouquet garni
1¼ cups white wine

MAKES 8 CUPS

Pick over the bones and discard any gut or oily fish. Soak and rinse, or run water over them until no blood is visible.

Meanwhile, heat the butter in a large, stainless steel or enamel Dutch oven, add the vegetables and herbs, and sauté gently for about 5 minutes. On no account let them brown.

Add the wine and bring to a boil. Add the drained fish bones. Cover with ice water and ice cubes if you have them, then skim off and discard the fat that congeals on the surface. Bring to a gentle simmer and cook for 30 minutes.

Strain into a bowl and let settle. Pour off the clear stock into a clean pan, discarding any residue. Boil to reduce the stock to about 8 cups, or until the flavor is as strong as you need. Transfer to convenient containers, about 1 cup each, then freeze.

Notes

• When making fish stock, never let the bones boil for more than 30 seconds, or they begin to dissolve their gelatin and the stock will become tacky when it is reduced to strengthen flavor.

• Sauté the vegetables in a little butter first to part cook them or they will not give up their flavor as quickly as the fish.

• When the vegetables and bones are covered with ice water, the cooking fat floats to the surface, solidifies, and can be lifted off and discarded. Ice cubes will make sure the water is cold enough to congeal the butter.

• Never add shellfish to an ordinary fish stock because you don't know who might be allergic to them. Keep a separate shellfish stock made from mussels, scallop trimmings, or the cooking water from lobsters or shrimp.

Safety Considerations

If casseroles are to be stored and reheated after cooking, this should be done carefully. The conditions in which food poisoning may occur are:

• When precooked food contains organisms, such as the staphylococcus organisms, which generate poisons.

• When cross-contamination occurs and food acquires harmful organisms transferred to it from unsterilized utensils, boards, and raw foods—the salmonella organisms.

The safest way to avoid food poisoning is to cook food from raw and then eat it right away while it is virtually sterilized. The elderly and very young should ideally be fed in this way, as their resistance to harmful bacteria tends to be low. However, with due care and attention to preventative procedures, there should be no problem with storing and reheating foods.

We ingest thousands of bacteria every day—some good, some bad—but trouble comes when we eat more of them than we can cope with over a short period.

There are two main situations in which this can occur. One is when food has been precooked, then kept in a warm environment: the other is when it has come into contact with dirty utensils or raw foods (which cannot be sterile), then left where the organisms can multiply.

Rule 1. Cooling

Cooked food should be cooled as soon as possible if it is not to be eaten immediately.

The cooking container should be lowered into a tub of ice water to reduce the temperature of the contents, especially stocks, as quickly as possible. This will reduce the length of time the contents are at a vulnerable temperature, typically between 160°F (about scalding point) and 40°F (the temperature of a cold refrigerator). There is an especially dangerous period at about 85°F (the temperature of a kitchen on a warm day) when bacteria, having landed on the cooked food, begin multiplying at an astonishing rate, doubling in number every few minutes. Dishes containing an amount of sugar or acid substances have a certain resistance to the problem, but are by no means immune.

Never put hot food in the freezer to cool quickly: this raises the temperature of the freezer and defrosts already frozen food.

Rule 2. Refrigerating

Once cool, stocks and meats should be covered and kept, for no more than 2 days, at or below 40°F—the recommended interior temperature for a domestic refrigerator—unless other forms of preservative have been employed.

After this time, meats and casseroles should be reheated and eaten. One of the bonus points here is that many casseroles benefit from this period of resting when flavors in the meats and liquids become interchanged and integrate into a more delectable whole.

The fat layer on stocks (other than poultry stocks, which have to be deep frozen) congeals at this temperature and may be lifted or scraped off prior to the stock being reduced.

Rule 3. Reheating

The temperature of wholesome food should be brought gently but steadily to a minimum 185°F all through if it is to be consumed immediately, and 212°F (boiling point) for 3 minutes when sterilizing stocks.

If the food is wholesome to be eaten cold, it will be wholesome when hot, if consumed at once. So, when you are reheating refrigerated food to eat immediately, there is no need to sterilize it. This may prevent overcooking, but will not guarantee to kill any salmonella present. However, if it has been stored correctly, there should not be sufficient numbers present to worry anybody but the very young or very old.

After this, food should preferably be discarded. Please note that cooked food that is not wholesome when eaten cold will not be wholesome just because it has been sterilized. The staphylococci organisms excrete poisons which are harmful and present in food even when boiled. Luckily,

salmonella is killed at boiling point and rendered harmless.

Rule 4. Freezing

Only freeze raw meats, poultry, fish, and vegetables and freshly cooked foods, stocks, and leftovers.

NEVER be tempted to think that freezing will preserve a questionable casserole or stock, or one that's been refrigerated for too long.

From this low temperature, the time taken to reheat it will give ample time for bacteria to multiply and become really poisonous. Apart from keeping cooked food for too long in a warm atmosphere, this is the most dangerous situation in which bacteria can multiply and excrete poison.

It is a good idea to divide stews and casseroles into manageable quantities of 2, 4, or 6 portions, as is convenient for your own requirements. This will prevent either wastage or the temptation to refreeze once-frozen items.

At freezer temperatures, evaporation of moisture still takes place, producing after an appreciable time a condition called "freezer burn" if items are not well wrapped or hermetically sealed. This is not poisonous, it just makes the food unpalatable and the burnt part should be cut away and discarded.

Certain foods, especially carbohydrates such as cooked rice, wheat flour, and potatoes, do not freeze well. Some raw meats and fish containing a lot of water in their cells also do not freeze well.

This is because water expands just below freezing point and breaks the cell walls, which deflate and release their water on thawing—a pity, but not poisonous. Sometimes, stirring the offending water into the gravy will help overcome the fault. Commercial blast freezing prevents this problem, but home freezers do not.

Casseroles and stocks should not be kept in a freezer for more than 4–5 months. After this time, the flavor and appearance deteriorate, although they will continue to be safe to eat.

Rule 5. Thawing

Cooked food should be given enough time to thaw completely in a cool place or refrigerator or microwave before being reheated. Stocks should be boiled from frozen.

Microwaving may speed things up, but you should make sure the center of the casserole reaches the required temperature before serving or before being finished off in a conventional oven. (Personally, I find this difficult to do without overcooking the outside.)

Index

conversion charts

Weights and measures have been rounded up
or down slightly to make measuring easier.

volume equivalents

american	metric	imperial
1 teaspoon	5 ml	
1 tablespoon	15 ml	
¼ cup	60 ml	2 fl.oz.
⅓ cup	75 ml	2½ fl.oz.
½ cup	125 ml	4 fl.oz.
⅔ cup	150 ml	5 fl.oz. (¼ pint)
¾ cup	175 ml	6 fl.oz.
1 cup	250 ml	8 fl.oz.

weight equivalents:

imperial	metric
1 oz.	25 g
2 oz.	50 g
3 oz.	75 g
4 oz.	125 g
5 oz.	150 g
6 oz.	175 g
7 oz.	200 g
8 oz. (½ lb.)	250 g
9 oz.	275 g
10 oz.	300 g
11 oz.	325 g
12 oz.	375 g
13 oz.	400 g
14 oz.	425 g
15 oz.	475 g
16 oz. (1 lb.)	500 g
2 1b.	1 kg

measurements:

inches	cm
¼ inch	5 mm
½ inch	1 cm
¾ inch	1.5 cm
1 inch	2.5 cm
2 inches	5 cm
3 inches	7 cm
4 inches	10 cm
5 inches	12 cm
6 inches	15 cm
7 inches	18 cm
8 inches	20 cm
9 inches	23 cm
10 inches	25 cm
11 inches	28 cm
12 inches	30 cm

oven temperatures:

225°F	110°C	Gas ¼
250°F	120°C	Gas ½
275°F	140°C	Gas 1
300°F	150°C	Gas 2
325°F	160°C	Gas 3
350°F	180°C	Gas 4
375°F	190°C	Gas 5
400°F	200°C	Gas 6
425°F	220°C	Gas 7
450°F	230°C	Gas 8
475°F	240°C	Gas 9